MAGIC IN THE MIDDLE

Magic in the Middle is your ultimate guide to creating a classroom filled with curiosity, collaboration, and creativity for gifted middle school learners!

Grounded in current research and enriched by years of hands-on classroom experience, this book provides 20 ready-to-use, practical lesson plans for gifted and high-ability learners. Each lesson is thoughtfully crafted to be culturally responsive, aligned with national gifted education standards, and adaptable to diverse learning needs. Centered around the theme of "middle school magic", every chapter is a transformative blend of movement, mystery, mingling, and made-to-order differentiation. These activities empower educators to move beyond screen-based learning, fostering active problem-solving, meaningful collaboration, and creative exploration.

Whether you're looking to spark joy, curiosity, or deeper intellectual engagement, *Magic in the Middle* equips educators at all career stages with the tools they need to balance academic rigor with the excitement of discovery. Visit www.routledge.com/9781041108634 for digital support resources and video teaching examples from the author!

Jessica L. LaFollette teaches gifted middle school students in Kansas City and graduate students at the University of Missouri. She is passionate about critical thinking and creativity in the classroom.

MAGIC IN THE MIDDLE

Hands-On Challenges That Create Joy for Middle School Gifted Learners

Jessica L. LaFollette

Routledge
Taylor & Francis Group
NEW YORK AND LONDON

Designed cover image: Getty Images

First published 2026
by Routledge
605 Third Avenue, New York, NY 10158

and by Routledge
4 Park Square, Milton Park, Abingdon, Oxon, OX14 4RN

Routledge is an imprint of the Taylor & Francis Group, an informa business

ISBN: 978-1-041-10864-1 (hbk)
ISBN: 978-1-041-10863-4 (pbk)
ISBN: 978-1-003-65716-3 (ebk)

DOI: 10.4324/9781003657163

Typeset in Chaparral Pro
by Apex CoVantage, LLC

Access the Support Material: www.routledge.com/9781041108634

To Brett and our girls who make my life magical

Contents

Introduction

It's 3:30 on a Monday afternoon and weirdly enough I can't stop smiling. My feet ache as I collapse into the chair at my desk and stare out the door where my students just left. Mentally I am exhausted but my heart is overflowing and somehow, I laugh out loud into the first silence I have experienced in several hours. Today was magical.

This elusive feeling of hope is why I love teaching. When a well-planned lesson comes together for the right students at the right time, there is an indefinable joy in the experience. As I look around the room, I see a few bits of paper, a broken pencil, and some chairs askew. It could be any middle school classroom on any afternoon, but wow, something really magnificent happened here. We never cracked open a student device, but there was a nearly constant buzz of curiosity and engagement in every class period today. The minutes flew by and I never sat down because the dialogue kept me just as engaged as they were. I know there was intense thinking going on, but there was also giggling, silliness, and occasionally an actual shout of excitement. They learned something new and important, then miraculously begged to

DOI: 10.4324/9781003657163-1

do it again. "How can I make that happen every day?" I think to myself.

Despite what others often believe, my gifted students are some of the most challenging learners in the building to teach. Ben is a brilliant seventh grader with ADHD who needs to move while he's thinking, couldn't care less about grades, and hates school on principle. Evelyn is a sweet and thoughtful sixth grader who will do anything teachers ask but is incredibly concerned about being wrong and wells up with tears when something is difficult for her. Zai is fourteen and his artistic talent leaves me speechless, but he refuses to fit into anyone's box and answers every question with sarcasm. Then there's the twelve-year-old twins Anthony and Mia, who have their entire lives mapped out from now through graduate school by their parents. They are always sure about the right answer but cannot bear to work with others who might slow them down. Kyla is a watchful and silent observer, more mature at age eleven than any of them, but has collected plenty of evidence that school is a waste of her time. Each of these extraordinary young humans are surrounded by my other neurodiverse thinkers, early finishers, and curious risk-takers. Middle school is a tough place and they all just want to find somewhere they can safely belong, have fun, and stretch their growing intellectual powers.

This book is for them and their teachers.

How To Make Magic

Do you believe in magic? Not the kind with wizards, fairy dust, or disappearing rabbits, but the deeper more psychosocial magic of a meaningful education. Every child deserves the kind of magic that makes them excited about learning something new and difficult. Every teacher deserves the kind of magic that fills our hearts with purpose and joy.

This perfect combination is elusive and difficult to replicate, especially with gifted learners who often start so far ahead of the curriculum designed for their typical peers. In this book, I'd like to introduce you to the four connected concepts that create magic for middle school gifted learners. When used regularly and carefully, they can make you and your students actually excited about coming to school.

Movement

The first magical concept is "Movement", defined as *kinesthetic and tactile learning* including physically manipulating objects in space and moving one's body around the room. Not only will this make your class immediately more exciting, it also makes it easier for young developing brains to learn complex material. These approaches are supported by decades of research (Sibley & Etnier, 2003) including recent studies specific to gifted education (Rakow, 2021; Rayneri et al, 2006). While empirical research on learning styles is mixed, the benefits of movement for all students is clear and especially for high-ability learners who may underachieve in a traditionally seated classroom environment. Recent neurological studies show that adolescent brains get more blood and are able utilize working memory more readily when they move their bodies rather than sitting still (Kjellenberg et al., 2024). This means that we cannot expect even our very bright students to absorb the most challenging concepts and skills while sitting at a desk or computer for an entire class period.

Planning for movement in the middle school classroom means letting go of a traditional seating chart with rows of desks that remain in the same positions for the entire school year. In this book, nearly every lesson involves movement around the classroom with students grouped in various formations and some lessons involve no seated activity at all. For a traditional teacher, this might feel like inviting chaos, but a few key procedures can easily keep things organized. First, allow free seating for your gifted students in various desk configurations early in the school year. Observe and then incorporate natural seating preferences of your learners (within reason) and develop seating rules as a class when they are needed. For example, an important seating rule in my classroom is that everyone must be in a chair at the front tables when the bell rings. Free seating is available later unless specific instructions are given otherwise.

A second helpful strategy for frequently incorporating movement is explicitly teaching and practicing seating transition routines. If you want to quickly go from partner tables to teams of four, students should know how and where to move their desks quickly. In my room, we often name the different table setups and practice transitioning with a timer or music. The final best practice for incorporating movement is to observe, listen, and reflect. Ask your students what is working for them and what seems to be making it more difficult to learn. Pay attention to comments and nonverbal cues then incorporate their suggestions to build buy-in.

If you're still not convinced about the magic of movement, go ahead and try it for yourself. Put this book down for a few minutes, get up and stretch your arms, legs, and neck. Walk around the room a few times, pick something up and move it around, or even try some jumping jacks if no one is watching. You'll enjoy and remember the next section more if you get more blood flowing to your brain!

Mystery

All human beings are born curious about the world around us. Children are especially thoughtful and excited about things that are novel, surprising, and mysterious. Unfortunately, traditional school has often suppressed if not eradicated much of this natural curiosity by the time kids reach middle school. Educators usually prefer and reward correct answers instead of genuine questions. The magic of engaging middle school gifted learners includes leaning into this concept of "Mystery", meaning *the unknown, curious, and potentially unanswerable.* Many of the lessons in this book include setting up situations, where genuine curiosity and authentic inquiry are rewarded and where students follow their instincts to investigate and solve challenging problems. Research with gifted middle school learners has found that significant epistemological differences exist between these students' development and that of their typical peers (Gallagher, 2019). These bright students who have more mature epistemological stances are likely to enjoy open-ended, inquiry-based tasks. They also have an ability to systematically organize facts and skills from various domains into meaningful connections.

To incorporate mystery into a lesson means to ignite curiosity with something surprising, then to build suspense, by encouraging questions over answers. As you facilitate a mysterious lesson, think about how your favorite suspenseful book or movie gives you just enough hints and excitement to leave you wanting more. If we want our students to be genuinely excited about solving problems and not give up when things are difficult, we have to stop handing them answers and allow them to ask questions, make guesses, and struggle through uncertainty. Even a miniscule mystery like guessing what is underneath a lumpy tablecloth or an overturned cup helps them wrestle with limited information and create meaningful hypotheses. Then they are better prepared to continue the ongoing productive inquiry of a longer-term investigation in other parts of our curriculum. They are also primed to generate more creative solutions.

One of the most difficult aspects of incorporating mystery is the need to customize the level of complexity so the solution is achievable but just enough out of reach to be intriguing. This is why lessons that would normally be appropriate in a middle school classroom often fall flat with gifted learners. When the solution is obvious, the mystery is lost and the only challenge remaining is to follow the teacher's directions. In the mysterious lessons of this book, I encourage you to start with the highest level of complexity your learners might possibly be able to tolerate. Tomlinson (2017) calls this teaching up, meaning we intentionally plan for the most advanced learners first. It is much easier to supplement the lesson with scaffolds and provide hints than it is to raise the mystery level mid-lesson.

Mingling

Another critical concept for middle school gifted lessons is "Mingling", which I will define as *productive communication and collaboration with a variety of peers*. I know you're probably thinking, "Oh yes, mingling means group work . . . but my gifted learners usually hate group projects!" Unfortunately, this is accepted as an incontrovertible truth by most educators who haven't experienced the magic of well-structured mingling. This is generally because gifted learners don't believe their ideas will be welcomed and/or they are expected to be the expert and handle most of the responsibilities of the group. When gifted learners are forced into an ill-defined group project with peers of mixed ability without learning mingling skills first, this will be the inevitable outcome.

However, collaboration and communication skills are essential for gifted children to be successful in almost any adult endeavor. Young adults with advanced intellectual abilities may or may not have advanced social skills and indeed often have social and emotional needs that differ from their typical peers (Galbraith & Delisle, 2015; Neihart, 2021). They have an important need like any other adolescent to feel a sense of belonging, but finding peers with whom they feel safe can be difficult. In your classroom of advanced learners, mingling should build a sense of trust between young adults who have expertise and skills in different areas. The lessons in this book incorporate intentional turn-taking for speaking and listening tasks as well as frequent opportunities for shared meaning-making. As I often tell my students, "The smartest person in the room is the room" (Weinberger, 2011), underscoring the fact that we are all much smarter when we recognize and listen to the varied expertise of others. When gifted middle school students are given frequent and varied opportunities to communicate and listen to intellectual peers with the goal of authentic collaboration, they become better equipped to handle the challenges of group work in a more heterogeneous setting.

Mingling means speaking, listening, and working together with a partner or a group. It also might look like shifting groups and collaborating with multiple different people during a single lesson. Sometimes a mingling lesson involves teamwork and competition, but most often the real goals are cooperation and collaboration. Similar guidance for successful movement in the classroom applies to effective mingling: observe and listen carefully to student needs, then customize the lesson expectations to address any concerns or avenues for growth.

Made-To-Order

The fourth and final concept that can truly make our middle school classrooms a magical place for gifted learners is "Made-To-Order", which is my way of emphasizing the critical importance of differentiating instruction. This means strategically customizing how we teach a lesson plan or unit of curriculum, based on the unique strengths and interests of the students in front of us (Roberts & Inman, 2023). In this book, I am explicitly encouraging you to alter my lessons! Using your professional expertise and a knowledge of your students' strengths and interests will be so much more effective than following my plans to the letter.

In a recent meta-analysis of differentiation practices used with high-ability learners, researchers highlighted the range of effective ways to tailor instruction including the use of higher-order thinking tasks, catering to interests, allowing for choice, and a range of flexible grouping and pacing practices (Nicholas et al., 2024). This was an important response to studies that show differentiation is misunderstood and often underutilized by classroom teachers who work with gifted learners, especially in middle school settings (VanTassel-Baska et al., 2020). The goal of this book is to provide practical examples of how to implement these effective differentiation practices in a middle school setting.

Another powerful practice that is directly connected to this made-to-order magic is culturally responsive teaching. Neurological studies prove that deep learning cannot take place when students feel disconnected, misunderstood, or even unsafe due to cultural or language differences (Hammond, 2014). Culturally responsive instruction gives us permission to listen to our students, take their needs seriously, and customize our teaching practices to address their unique strengths and interests (Fugate et al., 2021).

Throughout this book, I am delighted to offer practical ways to help you customize each of these great lesson plans to create your own made-to-order classroom magic. It helps that many of these lesson ideas are examples of low-floor, high-ceiling activities. This means they already allow plenty of room for your brightest and deepest thinkers to naturally move ahead when they are ready. However, I also provide concrete suggestions for customization that follow research-based, culturally responsive practices that are applicable to many different contexts. For example, I'll suggest when to provide or remove scaffolds, when to get input directly from students, and when to use their interests as the starting point. When we differentiate our instruction to match both ability and culture, we show our students we care about designing an experience specifically for them and the result is not just more meaningful learning but a growing trust that we value them as individuals.

Format and Goals of This Book

This book is designed to help busy middle school teachers effectively plan for their gifted and highly capable learners. It is not a work of curriculum. Instead, this book provides practical lesson ideas that should be incorporated into any type of curriculum when teachers are looking for a way to make their classroom experience more exciting, joyful, and hands-on. For example, when my students are conducting a rigorous problem-based inquiry they may spend several days researching and creating on their student devices, but I may also recognize the need for them to review key facts or share what they are learning with the group in an active and meaningful way. The lessons and strategies here allow expert educators to differentiate within any curriculum to meet the needs of our unique learners.

In each chapter, you will find a customizable lesson plan that lasts approximately one class period, is linked to national gifted education standards, and walks you through step-by-step facilitation of a hands-on activity. In addition to the lesson plan, each chapter contains a rationale, explaining when and how this lesson could be appropriate for your classroom as well as suggestions for customizing it to multiple types of content and group sizes. Following almost every lesson is a set of materials that are reproducible and "ready for Monday". If you find yourself in a pinch and need a hands-on and exciting lesson tomorrow, the resources are already prepared. Keep an eye out for this icon, which indicates when a resource is available for digital download at www.routledge.com/9781041108634.

At the end of this book, you'll find an appendix dedicated to assessment practices that are appropriate for these types of short-term hands-on lessons. Several flexible rubrics and checklists are provided for you to select the type of assessment and feedback that is most useful for you and your learners. Throughout the entire book I am also thrilled to share video examples of how these lessons look in action with real gifted learners as well as engaging ciphers to ignite your own curiosity.

Tech Time-out

How often do students use technology in your classroom? How often do they use it in the other six or seven classrooms they visit during the day? Since the global pandemic forced many educators to revolutionize delivery of content through digital instead of traditional lessons, middle schools have become places increasingly reliant on student devices and technology. The tools available online for teaching and learning are growing every day and can make learning more efficient and exciting, but they also often reduce the amount of movement, mystery and mingling that is possible within a given lesson. I am the first one to agree that technology use is an important and necessary part of preparing students for the future. In fact, we rely on digital tools for many aspects of highly effective curriculum in my gifted education classes. However, they are not the only or most effective way human beings can learn, communicate, or create. Unfortunately, the recent increases in adolescent screen time at home and school have been linked to negative consequences including adverse effects on language ability (Li et al., 2024), an increase in school-related stress, and a decrease in school satisfaction (Khan et al., 2022).

One of the primary goals of this book is to provide classroom ideas that do not require one-to-one student devices. They offer learners and teachers a chance to leave the Chromebooks and iPads packed away and rely instead on the knowledge and skills stored in the brain of every person in the room. Each lesson is designed to focus on active physical problem-solving and face-to-face communication. These skills are also desperately needed by our future leaders and innovators! Consider the lessons in this book as a tech time-out for your students. Offer them a chance to improve essential social skills and build confidence in critical thinking without the help of search engines or generative artificial intelligence. Two of the most powerful and magical lessons any bright child can learn are trusting their own brain to solve problems with a team and communicating their best ideas to others in a meaningful way.

The Most Important Lesson for Teachers

If you take nothing else away from the lessons here, I hope you appreciate that the most important component for magical learning is us! We have the power to turn on the mystery and allow a bit of movement and mingling. We know that learning new things should be exciting and fun for both teachers and students. If we are not feeling the joy and magic of education alongside our middle school students, they can absolutely sense our tired or reluctant attitude and will mirror it right back to us. When we are exhausted, checking things off a list, and focused on the "work" we have to do, we send a clear but unspoken message that school is a stressful kind of work to be endured at best. I know you have experienced that wonderful feeling of combining natural curiosity with cognitive strengths, or you wouldn't be teaching high-ability learners right now. I hope this book helps you find a little more of that magical feeling more often in your middle school classroom.

PLANNING THE MAGIC

Back at my teacher desk, I start to rethink my lesson plan for tomorrow. I was intending to have a quiet workday where students put content from their research projects onto slides. But, if I want another magical day like today, that lesson plan is not quite right. Ben will need to move around, Anthony and Mia need to hear some good ideas from others, and Zai needs a chance to let his sarcasm out before it winds up on the slides. Kyla and Evelyn need to know that we all really value hearing what they think. How can we do the important research, but also accomplish some other things they might need even more? I start to brainstorm ways that my plan for tomorrow can become more active and social. Maybe we can start with some movement and mingling, then I'll sneak in a mystery word that connects all their projects together. Instead of my Google Form exit ticket, they could share ideas out loud. Could we use a ball somehow or build something? What if there was a puzzle or code where they each had part of the solution from their research? As all these creative possibilities start to pop into my head, I realize I'm smiling again. Tomorrow is going to be another magical day.

Part I

Magic in a Moment

Ready To Teach in Ten Minutes or Less

It's Friday at 1 p.m. when the bell rings and Ben comes bounding into my room. After sitting still most of the day, he can't wait for my class where he hopes we might do something exciting. Beaming at me, he bounces enthusiastically on the exercise ball chair: "What are we doing today?" I can only shake my head and sigh because I am totally zapped of creative energy and just lost my planning time to cover someone else's class. To make matters worse, this group of students finished their project early yesterday and Evelyn has already emailed me concerned about when she'll get her score. I've got to come up with something great today to keep them engaged and learning without overtaking my other groups. It would also be nice to have a restful weekend, then my planning time on Monday to review their projects. If only there was something wonderful and quick that I could throw together while they work on the daily warm-up. They don't need busywork, just a straightforward challenging lesson to keep them engaged with content.

If this sounds familiar, the seven magical lessons here in Part I are ready to rescue you at the last minute. Each one is ready to go in less time than it takes to search TPT and print an overpriced set of worksheets. Better yet, your students will be moving, mingling, and thinking right away. None of these lessons requires expensive equipment or making copies. I have linked sample question sets and even instruction slides when they are needed. If your students enjoy these thinking challenges and want more, everything is easy to customize and reuse throughout the year with new content. So, take a deep Friday afternoon breath, and dive into the magic.

 DOI: 10.4324/9781003657163-2

Lesson 1

Around the World Divergent Thinking

Objective

Students will generate unique ideas while actively listening to each other.

Rationale

This magical lesson involves collaborative competition alongside a creative and physical memory challenge. It motivates my classes to actively listen to each other and give credit to each individual for sharing a new idea, while they work together at one of their favorite pastimes – outsmarting me! My stated goal is divergent thinking and they love to practice brainstorming creative ideas but it is often difficult for them to both generate new ideas and listen carefully to remember the ideas of others.

 DOI: 10.4324/9781003657163-3

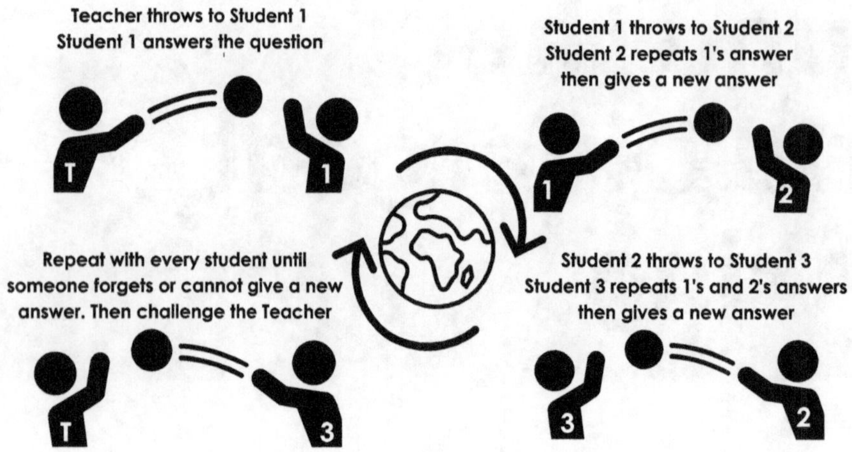

Figure 1.1 Around the World Divergent Thinking Process Diagram

They also don't often realize the social and emotional impact of having a peer make eye contact, say their name, and repeat their idea back. This happens again and again during this lesson and begins building classroom rapport and even friendships between casual acquaintances.

My students will almost never request to have a thoughtful discussion on a complex topic, because they are in middle school and thoughtful discussions are boring! But they will ask again and again to "play that game where we all throw the ball and try to beat you at answering the hard questions". This is my cue to get out the beach ball and cue up some deep questions. I hope you'll enjoy this activity with your classes as much as I do and along the way you'll learn something new about each learner as you toss the ball around the world.

Standards

NAGC 1.3. Self-Understanding. Students with gifts and talents demonstrate understanding of and respect for similarities and differences between themselves and their cognitive and chronological peer groups and others in the general population.

NAGC 4.2. Social Competence. Students with gifts and talents develop social competence manifested in positive peer relationships and social interactions.

NAGC 4.5. Communication Competence. Students with gifts and talents develop competence in interpersonal and technical communication skills. They demonstrate advanced oral and written skills and creative expression.

Preparation

Lesson Duration: 20–40 minutes

Materials Required: Set of open-ended questions, small lightweight ball

Background and Setup 5–10 minutes: Prepare slides with simple rules and a set of increasingly challenging open-ended questions. See **Resource 1.1: Around the World Memory Challenge** for an example. Inflate your ball if necessary.

Step-by-step Facilitation

1. Review the rules and answer any questions. Hold the ball in your hands as you do this to build anticipation.
2. Display a straightforward question on the board first for a practice round. I like to ask my students to name the best book they have read recently.
3. Toss the ball quickly to the first student who raises their hand.
4. This student simply shares their answer to the question and passes the ball to another student.
5. The second student must repeat the first student's name and answer, then share their own unique answer and pass the ball again.
6. The third student must repeat the first student's name and answer, the second student's name and answer, and then share their own unique answer before passing the ball to a new student.
7. Continue with this pattern until someone cannot remember a previous answer or cannot come up with a new answer. When this happens, they pass the ball back to the teacher for a challenge.
8. During the challenge, the teacher must correctly repeat all the students' names and answers in order as well as add their own new answer. If the teacher succeeds, they win the round and earn a point. If the teacher makes a mistake or cannot think of a new answer, the class wins the round and earns a point.
9. If the students can go "Around the World" by passing the ball, remembering and adding new answers until everyone has held the ball once, they automatically win and earn two points.

10. Repeat steps 2–9 with a new question. Increase the complexity and challenge of the questions each time.
11. Provide an exit ticket for reflection at the end of the lesson.

Tips for a Successful Lesson

- **Validating All Thoughtful Answers**

  When you ask students to come up with a new answer to a challenging question each time, you may get some far-fetched and unique ideas. This is when your class is really beginning to stretch their thinking. It will be important for you as the teacher to validate all thoughtful answers in order for this creativity to continue. You can say something like "Oh, that's really interesting!" or "Wow, what a creative answer". These simple comments will not slow the pace of the activity but encourage more students to think outside the box. If you want to discuss the answers more deeply, you can do so easily at the end of the round. (I have very few students ever offer incorrect or ridiculous answers when the entire class is listening so closely. They may think it will be funny one time, but when it is repeated again and again with their name attached, it quickly becomes embarrassing.)

- **It's Not Really About the Competition**

  Students will get very excited about remembering more than you or coming up with more creative answers. However, your ultimate goal is not to demonstrate your superior listening and thinking skills (which you undoubtedly have, given your age and experience) but instead to see their skills grow. Keep this in mind each time you are challenged and it will be easier to forgive yourself for making a mistake!

- **Strategies and Patterns**

  You may observe the class attempt to strategize and create a pattern to make the memory parts of this activity easier. They may decide to toss the ball only to the person sitting to their left or to try to go in the same order every time. Usually these attempts break down because I toss the ball quickly to a new person first each time. There is also frequently someone in the class who prefers to throw the ball as far as possible across the room to a friend rather than simply passing it to the left. I recommend allowing these strategies and discussing them before you decide to change the rules.

Assessment and Closure

At the end of the lesson, provide an exit ticket on a note card or sticky note asking students to respond to the following questions: Which question did you find the most interesting and why? Which was more difficult, remembering others' answers or coming up with a new answer? What question should the teacher ask next time we do this activity?

Differentiation Ideas

To provide additional thinking challenge, differentiate your questions by incorporating Kaplan's Depth and Complexity icons (2017). For example, instead of asking, "What makes someone a good leader?" approach the question using the multiple perspectives icon and restate it as, "How would citizens of ancient Rome view the qualities of a good leader compared to citizens of the current United States?" You can also provide more thinking and memory challenges within each question by asking students to justify their answer with an example or explanation. To differentiate the question "Who has been a great teacher in your life?" change it to, "Who has been a great teacher in your life and what is one thing you learned from them?" To provide additional scaffolding for struggling students, you can allow the use of dry-erase boards to take notes during the round or reduce the complexity of your questions.

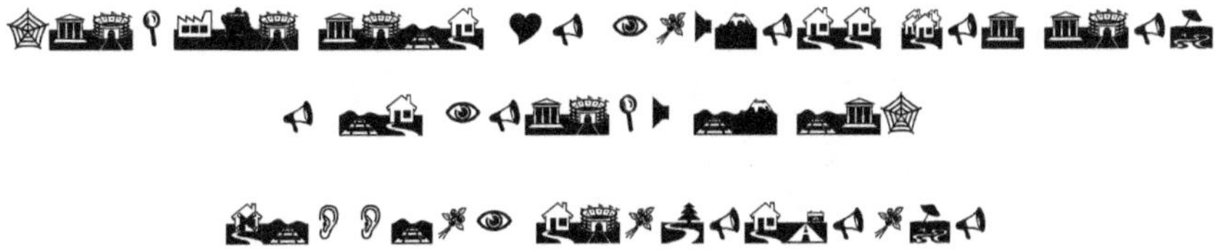

Make the Connection

Objective

Students will create four connected sets of terms, then correctly identify the connections created by peers and evaluate which connection patterns are the most challenging to solve.

Rationale

This is a critical thinking lesson that I taught digitally for a long time because it was incredibly convenient with a smart board and one-to-one student devices. However, I started to realize that convenience and speed were taking away from the deeper thinking and social connection that was actually possible within this creative challenge. It became a truly magical lesson when I adapted it to include physical

 DOI: 10.4324/9781003657163-4

movement, mingling, and dozens of short conversations with eye contact and laughter.

When you need a lesson that is very low-prep as well as low-floor, high-ceiling, this one checks all the boxes and will immediately engage your middle school students in a fun and joyful challenge. It requires nothing more than a big stack of note cards and an appetite for mystery. I hope you'll agree that spirited discussions over shades of meaning and the joy of experiencing a surprise connection are so much better than a silent room where everyone is focused on their own screen.

Standards

NAGC 3.5. Instructional Strategies. Students with gifts and talents become independent investigators.

NAGC 4.2. Social Competence. Students with gifts and talents develop social competence manifested in positive peer relationships and social interactions.

Preparation

Lesson Duration: 40–50 minutes

Materials Required: Note cards, Pencils, Physical objects from around the classroom (optional)

Background and Setup 5–10 minutes: Practice with PuzzGrid.com or the *New York Times* free daily Connections game for inspiration and to experience the thrill of successfully finding links between seemingly unrelated terms. Prepare enough small blank cards so every pair of students will have 17. Select or create your own example puzzle to start the lesson.

Step-by-step Facilitation

1. Start with an example puzzle grid on the board with 16 terms, where only you know the correct four groups of four related terms.
2. Ask students to raise their hands if they see four words that all have a connection. When you call on them, make sure to ask them what the four words have in common.

3. If they are correct, select or cross out the completed terms, then ask for another connection.
4. When the class has solved the entire puzzle, announce that today they will be creating their own connection puzzles.
5. Divide students into partners and distribute 17 cards to each pair of students.
6. Allow time for student pairs to work, secretively choosing four sets of four words that have a connection and using their best handwriting to label the 16 cards. The 17th card should contain an answer key and the creators' names.
7. As students are working, move throughout the room, checking and assisting as necessary. Try your best to preview each connection and answer key for accuracy and legibility.
8. Students should arrange the cards into a four-by-four grid with all 16 terms mixed up and flip their answer key face down.
9. When everyone has created a complete grid and flipped their note card answer key, ask one student from each pair to stand up.
10. The standing student should rotate to a neighboring desk to attempt to solve another group's connection puzzle. The seated student remains at the puzzle they created to check the work of those moving around the room.
11. Students should have about three minutes at each puzzle to attempt to solve it. Set a timer if needed to keep them moving. When one group of four terms is guessed correctly the creator removes those cards from the grid and groups them together at the top. Once a puzzle is completely solved or the time is up, the creator is responsible for resetting the grid for the next player.
12. When the standing students have finally rotated back to their own puzzle they sit down and swap roles with the seated student.
13. Continue the three-minute rotations until everyone has had a chance to attempt every puzzle in the room.
14. Collect all stacks of cards and answer keys, then debrief with the class. What types of puzzles were the easiest and most difficult to solve? What were some of the most surprising connections and trickiest red herrings invented by the class? What makes a connection puzzle a good combination of challenging and fun? What makes a puzzle so frustrating that you don't want to keep trying to solve it?

Tips for a Successful Lesson

- **Proceed with Caution**

  For the teacher, step 7 is critical but tempting to skip because students will be working so intently you may not want to interrupt. However, there will often be one or two students who try to use words that are either inappropriate for school or way too specific and difficult for most other students in the class to understand. Remind these creators that the goal is to create a set of connections that is both challenging and fun for the entire class including any visitors like parents or the principal. Also, be prepared that there may be some totally appropriate connections that most or all of your middle school class will understand and you may not! This is a great time for you to learn new slang and brush up on the unique pop culture interests of your learners.

- **Refining and Revising**

  As students rotate around the room it may become apparent to certain creators that they have made aspects of their puzzles too difficult or too simple. Some students may even come to the shocking revelation that others cannot read their handwriting! This is a natural and wonderful part of getting immediate peer feedback. It is completely fine to pause the rotation of solvers and allow all the groups a few minutes to "refine and revise" their puzzles before resuming.

Assessment and Closure

After the debrief, ask each student to score themselves on a critical thinking rubric. On the back of the rubric ask students to list the names of the creators of the puzzle that was the most challenging and fun to solve.

Differentiation Ideas

There are many additional ways to customize this activity to your current curriculum or to the individual needs of students. To make the lesson more challenging and require students to think carefully before guessing, you can implement a "three strikes" rule. This means anyone who guesses three times *in a row* incorrectly can no longer attempt the puzzle. I advise increasing the thinking time from three to five minutes if you apply this rule and often this is only fair to do after they have completed this lesson at least once.

An extension that requires deeper thinking and additional creativity is moving beyond words and cards to physical objects. Similar to the memory display lesson, students select 16 objects from their backpacks or around the classroom and set them up in a grid. These objects' connections can be physical or metaphorical, which really increases the challenge!

If your students struggle to create puzzles, try providing a deck of cards from any other game in your classroom. Students can often create four connected groups much faster this way. You can also lower the number of connections required to three sets of three terms.

If students are struggling to solve the puzzles, allow creators to give up to two hints per student or to remove one of the groups right at the beginning. Another fun adaptation for all levels is to allow students to solve puzzles created by other classes and then vote on their favorites to submit online. The Puzzgrid website allows you to log in and create digital versions of these puzzles that can be played anytime.

Example Puzzle 1 Created by an Adult:

Nurse	**Dog**	**Ant**	**Blood**
Super	**Locust**	**Sand**	**Top Hat**
Bat	**Frog**	**Hammerhead**	**Boot**
Tiger	**Thimble**	**Boil**	**Spider**

Example Puzzle 2 Created by Two Gifted Middle School Students:

The inBESTigators	**Coconuts**	**Orange**	**High Potential**
Strawberry	**Drizella**	**Will Trent**	**Tomato**
Fire Truck	**Palm Tree**	**Gronk**	**Pluto**
Manatee	**Lady**	**Perry the Platypus**	**Apple**

ANSWER KEY

Puzzle 1 Answers: Sharks (Nurse, Tiger, Sand, Hammerhead); Heroes ending with -man (Super, Ant, Bat, Spider); Biblical Plagues (Frog, Blood, Boil, Locust); Monopoly Pieces (Dog, Top Hat, Boot, Thimble)

Puzzle 2 Answers: TV Crime Fighters (The inBESTigators, Perry the Platypus, High Potential, Will Trent); Red Things (Strawberry, Tomato, Fire Truck, Apple); Obscure Disney Characters (Drizella, Pluto, Lady, Coconuts); Things you find in Florida (Orange, Gronk, Manatee, Palm Tree)

Lesson 3

Counting Concentration

Objective

Students will communicate nonverbally to collaboratively name 20 concepts in a known sequence.

Rationale

Have you ever wondered if your middle school gifted students actually know how to listen to each other carefully without interrupting? The development of this social skill may not follow at the same pace as their advanced cognitive skills (Silverman, 2017) and they might truly need to practice. In this made-to-order lesson, your students will collaborate to successfully name several concepts in order while only one person can

DOI: 10.4324/9781003657163-5

speak at a time and only name one thing. The magic at work here is in the mingling of thoughts, ideas, and strategies through both verbal and non-verbal communication.

Your students will likely find this challenge frustrating at first, so they will also be rehearsing collective resiliency and determination to succeed. These skills will serve them throughout many other class projects and future endeavors outside of school. You may have observed that it is very difficult for some bright students to wait patiently for others to speak when they know the correct answer. This act of patient listening is a skill that must be practiced too. Your job as the facilitator of this lesson is merely to listen carefully and offer meaningful encouragement when they inevitably have to start over again and again. You can also prepare to joyfully cheer out loud with the entire group when they finally name the last concept on the list without making a mistake!

Standards

NAGC 4.2. Social Competence. Students with gifts and talents develop social competence manifested in positive peer relationships and social interactions.

NAGC 4.5. Communication Competence. Students with gifts and talents develop competence in interpersonal and technical communication skills. They demonstrate advanced oral and written skills and creative expression.

Preparation

Lesson Duration: 20–30 minutes

Materials Required: None

Background and Setup 5 minutes: Select a set of approximately 20 concepts that your students should be able to name in order from memory. Take the 20 concepts directly from your current curriculum or start with the basic numbers, counting numbers one to twenty.

Step-by-step Facilitation

1. Divide the class into groups of five to ten students.
2. Each group should form a standing circle so all students can clearly see and hear each other.

3. For practice, allow each group to count from one to twenty in unison (or name the entire sequence of concepts together). If they struggle with this as a group, allow a few extra rounds of practice.
4. When the concentration round begins, students must speak one person at a time in a random order. Each person may state only one number or concept at a time and all students must speak at least once. If two students speak at the same time, or if anyone accidentally says something out of order, the entire group must start again. They may not say any words aloud other than the numbers or concepts they are listing.
5. Repeat until the group can successfully name all 20 in order without making a mistake.
6. When each small group has successfully completed the challenge at least once, combine the entire class into one large group and attempt the concentration round again. If you have more than 20 students, you may need to drop the rule that everyone has to speak and replace it with a rule that no one can speak more than once.
7. The students should be slightly better at eye contact and listening after working with a small group, but this challenge is much more difficult with a large number of people. Repeat the process until the entire class can successfully name all 20 in order without making a mistake.
8. Debrief by discussing the difficulty of this challenge and what ultimately helped them to be successful. What types of nonverbal cues did they give each other? Did they come up with a pattern or another strategy? How did it feel to only listen, when you wanted to speak? Close the class with an exit ticket that asks students to name a successful nonverbal strategy they used to communicate with their peers.

Tips for a Successful Lesson

- **Choosing Concepts to Name**

  If you'd like to select something other than counting numbers to give your students a real challenge, consider concepts that are worth memorizing and knowing for the rest of their lives. This memory activity is really that powerful! All learners can benefit from learning to count in a foreign language and often a bilingual student in your class can easily lead this activity.

History students can memorize the presidents of the U.S., math students can learn the Fibonacci sequence, or science students can learn the first 20 elements of the periodic table. This activity is also a wonderful way to help students memorize poetry. I recommend "Nothing Gold Can Stay" by Robert Frost, which has exactly 40 words and provokes a deep discussion every time.

- **Gestures, Ordering, and Other Strategies**

  Inevitably your students will seek and find a strategy together to conquer this concentration challenge. I have seen all kinds of ingenious strategies such as taking a loud breath before speaking, winking one eye, or even a simple head nod. Some students can even come up with a complex pattern of going around the circle but skipping two students every time – all without actually discussing the strategy out loud. It is up to you how strict you want the requirement for randomness to be for your group. I have occasionally added a rule that everyone must look directly down at the ground to increase the challenge. However, my social objective in this lesson is usually for them to learn to listen to each other and to improve their nonverbal communication skills, so I typically allow these little gestures and patterns to develop naturally. Then we discuss them as a group and why they are useful in other situations.

Assessment and Closure

After the debrief and discussion, close the class with an exit ticket that asks students to name a successful nonverbal strategy they used to communicate with their peers. Analyze these tickets for strategies that were not named. These are the skills that may need to be taught more directly. Follow up this lesson with an individual content-based assessment if you are using named concepts rather than the numbers one to twenty. Your students will be excited to prove how many they can correctly remember in the right order!

Differentiation Ideas

To provide additional challenge for your advanced nonverbal communicators, require them to close their eyes or look at the floor as described previously. Increasing the group size also instantly raises the level of challenge.

Another rule that increases the challenge is to have students switch positions in the circle every time they restart and/or requiring a new starting speaker each time.

For any neurodivergent students who may be struggling with small nonverbal cues or staying focused, provide a card of hints for what to look for in the other players. You can also suggest small movements they can do to signal to the group that they want to speak next such as taking a small step forward or one deep breath. Alternatively, suggest that this student start the group off each time.

Lesson 4

What's My Pattern?

Objective

Students will create and identify a pattern or sequence and predict the next term. Then they will evaluate which patterns are the most challenging to solve and defend their choice.

Rationale

When you need a speedy lesson that requires students to think deeply and gives them a chance to move around the room, this activity provides all the magic for high levels of engagement. It requires almost no prep on your part, but instead asks students to do the thinking. It works because our students' brains are always looking for patterns and meaning while

 DOI: 10.4324/9781003657163-6

also seeking social connection (Willis, 2008). Each pair of students creates their own mystery and gets a chance to solve the mysteries of others in the class. They also get to use playing cards in class, which always levels up the excitement.

This is one of the best examples in this book of low-floor, high-ceiling learning experiences. Any pair of students can create a simple numerical or color pattern from a deck of cards, but students with advanced cognitive abilities will see and share all kinds of other patterns. Of course, gifted learners need an opportunity to think at this high level, but they also need practice explaining their reasoning to others. This lesson allows everyone in the class to practice switching perspectives and roles.

Start by considering your students' level of comfort with mathematical patterns and sequences. By middle school all students should be familiar with skip counting and other basic arithmetic sequences. However, some advanced math students will have had exposure to geometric patterns and even more complex sequences like Fibonacci's. If you teach math or want to provide direct instruction on geometric sequences prior to this lesson, your students will naturally create more advanced patterns. Don't worry though, even if you don't teach advanced math, students will be excited to show off their pattern creating skills and teach you what they know.

Standards

NAGC 3.5. Instructional Strategies. Students with gifts and talents become independent investigators.

NAGC 4.2. Social Competence. Students with gifts and talents develop social competence manifested in positive peer relationships and social interactions.

Preparation

Lesson Duration: 20 – 45 minutes

Materials Required: 1 deck of playing cards per student or pair, slides introducing the game and providing examples (See **Resource 4.1 What's My Pattern** for a customizable example), note cards

Background and Setup 5–10 minutes: Customize slides if desired. Review mathematical patterns and sequences if necessary.

Step-by-step Facilitation

1. Provide a deck of cards and one blank note card to every student or pair of students.

2. Allow a minute or two for students to open the deck, shuffle it, spread them out, etc.
3. Introduce the game and the rules using the slides.
4. Ask students to replicate the pattern example from the slides then add the correct fifth card.
5. Walk through the room to confirm that everyone understands the rules and the simple example patterns.
6. Ask students to create their own new pattern of four cards.
7. Next, they will describe the pattern and the correct fifth card on the note card then flip it over. This is the answer key.
8. As students are working, move throughout the room, checking and assisting as necessary. Try your best to preview each pattern for accuracy.
9. On the table should be four cards in order from left to right, a stack of unused cards, and a completed answer key note card turned face down.
10. When everyone has created a pattern and flipped their note card answer key, ask students to stand up.
11. Now they may move to any desk that isn't their own to attempt to solve another student's pattern.
12. When they think they have the correct answer, they should pull the fifth card from the stack and lay it at the end of the group of four, then raise their hand.
13. Move to each student with a hand raised to check their answers using the key on the note card. (You may collect these note cards if you feel there could be a temptation to cheat.)
14. If you confirm the correct answer, they should hide the correct card and move to another table.
15. Students should continue moving and working until most of the class has solved most of the patterns. If there is a particularly tricky problem where multiple students are getting stuck, you may ask the patternmakers to give a hint.
16. Return to original seats and repeat with every student or pair now creating a new pattern. They should have several new ideas from solving each other's patterns.
17. Repeat Round 2 as you did Round 1. Provide new note cards if needed.

Tips for a Successful Lesson

- **Face Cards and Suit Names**

  Not all students will have had an equal opportunity to use a standard deck of playing cards. A quick and simple review of the suit names and value of the face cards is always appropriate the first time you try this activity. I believe it is easiest if the ace cards represent the number one, but you can change this rule if you choose. If needed, display a key on the board during the entire lesson.

- **Repetition**

  This lesson is the most meaningful on round two and beyond. This is the time when everyone has had a chance to observe and consider the unique ideas of their classmates and incorporate those into a new and more challenging pattern. At some point, repeating patterns will emerge from two different groups. I believe it is important here to emphasize the value of emulating a strong pattern without copying it directly. Give students time to discuss and defend their similar patterns, carrying them out past the number of cards available in the deck. Are the patterns truly identical? How does understanding one pattern give you clues to solving the next pattern? The answers to these questions can carry the discussion and applicability of this lesson far beyond mathematics.

- **Rotating Responsibility**

  Instead of allowing all students to travel while you check answers, you can alternate who travels around the room and who stays at the pattern mystery to discuss it with others. These opportunities to mingle and communicate with multiple other students are part of the magic in this lesson. There will always be a few students who prefer to sit and guard the puzzle and others who prefer to move around, but in order for them to have an equal opportunity to learn from each other and practice communication skills, both partners must rotate these responsibilities.

Made-to-order Mystery Patterns Beyond Playing Cards

This lesson fits perfectly into a middle-level math enrichment class when using standard playing cards. However, it can be extended and incorporated far beyond a math class if you have several sets of cards with a clear sequence of values. For example, timeline cards from a period in history can be ordered and used to create mystery patterns. In science class, try cutting up a colorful periodic table to make an excellent deck of cards for this activity. Music notes or solfège terms can also create all kinds of fun patterns to be sung or played on an instrument. You can also try alphabetizing complex vocabulary terms and writing them on colorful paint chips. Once your students begin learning to look for patterns, they will really start to see them everywhere!

Assessment and Closure

Exit ticket is the note card answer key with an evaluation and analysis question. "Which pattern was the most challenging to solve and why?"

Differentiation Ideas

To make the game easier, increase the number of playing cards in each pattern to five. To extend a student's thinking, ask students to write a mathematical definition of the nth term in the sequence.

Lesson 5

Trashketball

Objective

Students will review or preview content knowledge while building social competence and teamwork skills.

Rationale

This lesson is a middle school favorite for obvious reasons. They love getting permission to throw something and the rules of the game equally reward both academic and athletic skills. Even my most reluctant students get excited about playing trashketball. The magic here is in the combination of challenging thinking, active movement, and mingling within the group. This particular set of trashketball rules is designed to encourage maximum collaboration within a population of bright learners who often prefer to work

 DOI: 10.4324/9781003657163-7

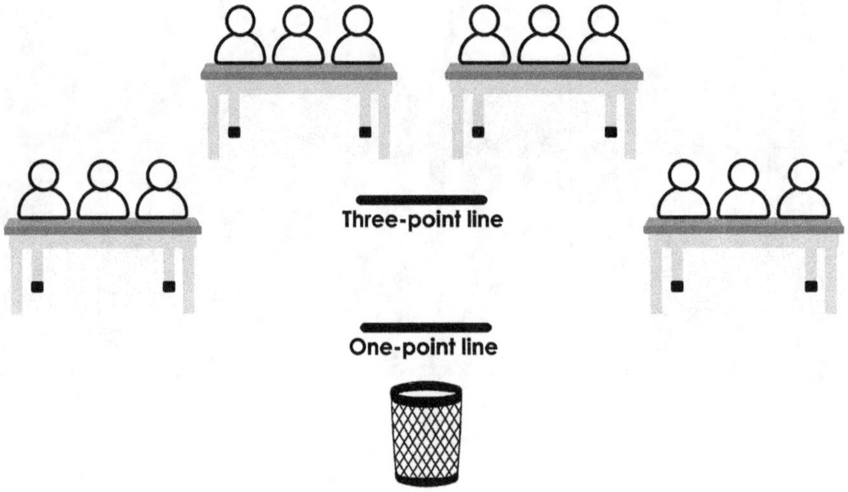

Figure 5.1 Trashketball Classroom Setup

independently. When they are required to discuss their answers so everyone can explain it if needed, they learn to depend on each other. When there is a chance to throw a ball across the room they double- and triple-check their answers to every difficult question. It is highly motivating and really fun!

Trashketball is an excellent high-energy lesson to keep in your back pocket for anytime you have an extra 15 minutes. Once students have been taught the rules (and you've allowed them to create some custom house rules) they can help you set it up in less than a minute. If you have a challenging set of questions prepared and want to encourage collaborative discussion, I think you'll find that trashketball is so much more effective and engaging than almost any other form of review, including online gaming platforms.

Standards

NAGC 4.2. Social Competence. Students with gifts and talents develop social competence manifested in positive peer relationships and social interactions.

Preparation

Lesson Duration: 10–30 minutes

Materials Required: Empty trash can, Small lightweight ball, Dry-erase boards, Markers and erasers, Question set, Painter's tape, Music that can be started and stopped quickly (optional).

Background and Setup 5–10 minutes: Select a set of challenging questions. Place the empty trash can at the front of the room, not against a wall. Measure and mark a one-point and a three-point line on the floor with painter's tape. Test with your selected ball and adjust as needed. The one-point line should be pretty easy to shoot from for any student, while the three-point line should be a good challenge.

Step-by-step Facilitation

1. Divide the class into teams of two to four students.
2. Distribute one dry-erase board, marker, and eraser to each team.
3. Start a scorekeeping tally.
4. Read questions aloud.
5. Play music while all groups discuss and write an answer on their boards.
6. Stop the music and ask all groups to show their answers at once.
7. Scan the room and announce the correct answer. Save the question to repeat if few or no teams know the correct answer.
8. Each team with a correct answer earns one point and selects a team member to shoot.
9. The first person to shoot must explain how they came up with the answer or provide a justification. Rotate this opportunity between each team if possible.
10. Each eligible shooter gets to select the one-point or three-point line and try for a "Trashket".
11. If they make the shot, add the appropriate number of points to their team score.
12. Repeat with the next question and continue until all content has been reviewed.
13. Provide exit tickets for self-reflection.

Tips for a Successful Lesson

- **One Correct Answer Please**

  Choose a set of questions that each have a single clearly correct answer. I find this activity works really well with a high-level math or science review. (If you want an active lesson to encourage divergent thinking, check out the chapter called "Around the World".) Start with the easier questions, then slowly raise the level of complexity as high as possible to really stretch their thinking. They will become more motivated as they get a chance to shoot more baskets.

- **Choose a Small Lightweight Ball**

  A foam or beach ball works very well for this activity because you don't want it to damage anything as it bounces off the rim of the trash can. You can also use balled up paper if needed. The ball should be easy for students to throw and an appropriate size for the clean trash can you are using as a basket.

- **Let Them Strategize**

  When the rules are clear, teams will naturally begin to collaborate and strategize to maximize their points. When you don't require everyone to take a shot, they feel more comfortable choosing to take the chance when they are ready. When you ask the first team who wants to shoot to explain how they got the correct answer, their confidence blossoms right before their big moment. There is magic in learning to appreciate each teammate's unique skills. Listen closely to how they recognize and play to each other's strengths. Congratulate teams who figure out what works best for their group even if they aren't leading in the points. These collaborative social skills will carry on far beyond this simple activity.

- **Good Sportsmanship**

  Take this opportunity to clearly teach some important life skills related to competition. Be very clear that "trash talk" is not allowed in trashketball. They will get excited and want to cheer when they get an answer correct or when a teammate makes a shot. This should absolutely be encouraged! The pure joy on a student's face when their peers cheer for them is priceless. However, it is never okay for students to berate each other for making a mistake. Practice beforehand by missing a few shots yourself and rehearsing an appropriate response that can express disappointment but also be encouraging at the same time.

Made-to-order Movement

The possibilities to customize trashketball are nearly endless. It is most effective when you start simple, then allow students to suggest some creative house rules or give input on any changes you want to make. If you do change a rule or the setup, ask students to provide input after playing a few rounds. Take a class vote on whether the changes made the game better or worse. The one thing I never compromise on is the difficulty of the questions. Thinking at a high level is the most important component to any successful lesson for gifted learners!

Trashketball Variations

- Use paper from your recycling bin for students to write the answers then crumple the paper into a ball to throw.
- Allow students to invent an optional five-point or ten-point shot.
- Use trashketball to go over paper homework questions or test items. Each time a team shoots and scores, they give up a paper to the recycling bin.
- When several teams answer correctly, allow the first shooter to select any place in the room to make a shot, then each following team must shoot from that same place.
- If only one team answers a question correctly allow them to have two shots.
- When one team is leading by a large margin, double the point values for a more dramatic “final round”.

Assessment and Closure

Exit ticket on note card or sticky note. What is your personal strength during trashketball? Answering questions? Shooting baskets? Encouraging others? Strategy? Name one other person from your team and their personal strength during trashketball.

Differentiation Ideas

For advanced learners, increase the difficulty of the questions or shorten the amount of time to think and discuss the answers. To provide support, add multiple-choice answers to your questions or increase the amount of discussion time. You may also consider posting each question on an individual slide to display rather than simply reading them aloud.

Sample Trashketball Question Set
Mathematics and Problem-solving

(Similar to ACT/SAT questions: Calculators Encouraged)

1. Lalani took four tests, scoring: 100, 60, 85, and 92. Then she took a fifth test. The mean score of the five tests she took is 87. What was her score on the fifth test?
   a. 98

2. The initial speed of a car that skids to a stop can be estimated by multiplying the length of the skid by 35 and then taking the square root of the product. According to this method, what is the estimated initial speed of a car when its skid measures 58?
   a. 45

3. In △ABC, ∠A and ∠C are congruent, and the measure of ∠B is 123°. What is the measure of ∠A?
   a. 28.5°

4. Brett brought some chips and candy to share with the class on his birthday. Each member of the class received the same number of chips and the same amount of

candy. The total number of pieces of candy he gave to the class was 30, and the total number of chips was 75. What is the greatest number of classmates Brett could possibly have?

a. 15

5. If $12y = 7x - 1$, then $x = ?$

a. $x = (12y + 1) / 7$

6. Hope is traveling in a speedboat on a lake at 45 miles per hour. How fast is she traveling in feet per second? (1 mile = 5,280 feet)

a. 66

7. Thirty ping-pong balls are numbered with the integers 1 through 30 and placed in a bin. One ball will be randomly drawn from this bin. What is the probability that this ball will have a prime number on it?

a. 10/30 or 1/3

8. An airplane leaves Kansas City at 2 p.m. and flies directly north at 250 miles per hour. A second airplane leaves Kansas City exactly 30 minutes later and flies north at 280 miles per hour. At what time will the second plane overtake the first?

a. 6:40 p.m.

9. Solve this system of equations for x

$2x + y = 7$
$x - 2y = 6$

a. $x = 4$

10. Amelia had \$80 in her savings account. When she received a paycheck from her first job, she deposited some money and brought her balance up to \$120. By what percentage did she increase her savings?
    a. 50%

Sample Trashketball Question Set Animal and Plant Cell Structure and Function

1. What structure controls the activities of the cell?
   a. Nucleus

2. Name the jellylike substance in which chemical reactions take place.
   a. Cytoplasm

3. Most cells contain this structure that releases energy.
   a. Mitochondria

4. Plant cells contain this structure to strengthen the cells.
   a. Cell Wall

5. What structure is needed by plant cells to perform photosynthesis?
    a. Chloroplasts

6. This structure controls which substances can enter or exit the cell.
    a. Cell membrane

7. What is the general name for smaller structures that carry out different functions within the cell?
    a. Organelles

8. Which cell structure forms a maze of passageways for materials to move around the cell?
    a. Endoplasmic reticulum

9. A water-filled sac inside the cell that acts as a storage area.
    a. Vacuole

10. Structures that receive proteins from the endoplasmic reticulum and package them up to distribute to other parts of the cell.
    a. Golgi bodies

Lesson 6

Fishbowl

Objective:

Students will review a set of concepts by communicating verbally and nonverbally.

Rationale:

Communication skills involve not just speaking and writing, but also nonverbal and paraverbal abilities like eye contact, gestures, inflection and intonation. In this magical lesson, your students will laugh, shout, and sit silently on the edges of their seats waiting to respond to only a tiny word or movement. I love this activity because it is a wonderful combination of higher-level thinking, physical movement, student-generated mystery,

DOI: 10.4324/9781003657163-8

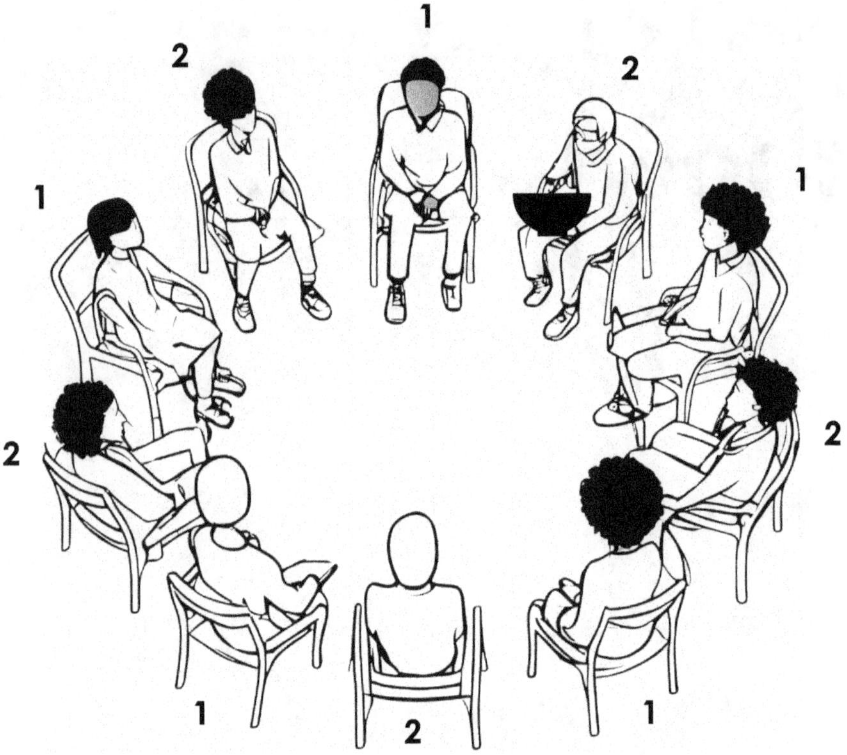

Figure 6.1 Fishbowl Classroom Setup in Teams

safe mingling within teams and a large group, and customized made-to-order content.

Fishbowl is another example of a low-floor, high-ceiling lesson where students can set the bar for themselves. It involves almost no prep time for the teacher and can be accomplished in any classroom environment with at least four students. Keep in mind that the joy it incites in a group is contagious and you may find yourself smiling and chuckling long after school because of the creative descriptions, motions, and sounds your students will come up with in this lesson.

Standards

NAGC 4.2. Social Competence. Students with gifts and talents develop social competence manifested in positive peer relationships and social interactions.

NAGC 4.5. Communication Competence. Students with gifts and talents develop competence in interpersonal and technical communication skills. They demonstrate advanced oral and written skills and creative expression.

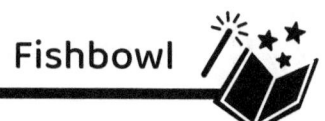

Preparation

Lesson Duration: 30–60 minutes

Materials Required: One large plastic bowl, at least two small slips of construction paper per student, writing utensils, 30-second digital or sand timer

Background and Setup 5–10 minutes: Cut colorful paper into small strips approximately 1 cm × 4 cm or ask a student helper to do this for you. Notebook paper and white printer paper is easy to see through, so I recommend using construction paper or cardstock. Make sure you have at least two slips of paper per student. Arrange chairs into a circle or U-shape so students can easily make eye contact with everyone else in the room. Present a set of slides with simple rules for each round. See **Resource 6.1 Fishbowl** for a customizable example.

Step-by-step Facilitation

1. Seat the entire class in a large circle where they have some room to move and everyone can see and hear each other clearly.
2. Pass out two blank slips of paper to each student and make sure everyone has a writing utensil.
3. Instruct students to write ONE WORD on each slip of paper that is related to the content you are currently studying. Emphasize these three precautions as students write their words:
    a. Use neat handwriting and correct spelling. Try printing in all capital letters.
    b. Make sure your word is something everyone has heard of and something you would be willing to act out.
    c. Only school-appropriate words are allowed.
4. Collect the completed slips and check for duplicates as you fold them and place them into the fishbowl.
5. Inform students that the class is already divided into two teams. The two people sitting next to them on their right and left are members of the opposing team, while their teammates are sitting one person away. If you have an odd number of students, you may appoint one person to play on both teams. To help students recognize their teammates, designate one person as team "1", then ask all members of team 1 to raise their hands. The students not raising their

hands are team "2". Students should look around carefully to see who is on their team.

6. Hold the fishbowl in your hand as you review the simple rules on the board for each round. All rounds are conducted with the same set of words.
   a. Round one is like the game Taboo. Students can say any words except the word on the paper or any part of that word. Rhyming and spelling are also not allowed.
   b. Round two is like the game Charades where students must act out the word with no speaking or sounds.
   c. Round three is like the game Password where students can only say one word or sound to get their team to correctly guess the word on the paper. No gestures are allowed in round three.
7. During each round, students will pass the fishbowl around the circle, drawing a new slip of paper to use each time they receive the bowl. They have 30 seconds to get their teammates to guess the word correctly or it goes back into the bowl. If the team gets the answer right, the student keeps the slip of paper and immediately passes the bowl.
8. The timer should be held and restarted every 30 seconds by one responsible student for the entire round.
9. The round ends when the fishbowl is empty. Teams tally up their total points then place all the papers back into the bowl.
10. Repeat steps 7–9 for each round. The team with the highest total at the end of all three rounds is the winner.
11. Close the lesson with an exit ticket asking students to write a word or concept reviewed today that they did not know much about before the class, but now will probably never forget and why.

Tips for a Successful Lesson

- **Check Every Slip**

  As students hand you their handwritten papers, check each one carefully before it goes into the bowl. My biggest issues are duplicates and messy handwriting. When this happens, I hand them back a blank slip and ask for a quick redo. Every once in a while, someone tries to turn in something that is inappropriate or spelled so strangely it is illegible. In this case, I ask a few questions to find out what they actually meant and suggest some alternatives. This step is easy to skip but prevents so much drama later that it is worth the extra few minutes before starting the activity.

- **Passing**

  You may want to include a rule about passing if someone is holding the bowl and draws a word they do not know or cannot figure out how to describe or act out for the team. I suggest allowing one pass per person per round, but they must draw a new paper and attempt that one in place of the word they wish to pass. The passed word should go back into the bowl so someone else can attempt it.

Assessment and Closure

Close this lesson with an exit ticket asking students to write a word or concept reviewed today that they did not know much about before the class, but now will probably never forget and why. Conduct your own assessment of student thinking skills during the fishbowl rounds using a rostered student checklist. Use this data to determine which thinking skills need to be reviewed in another activity. Finally, conduct a review of the concepts represented in the list of words students selected to place into the fishbowl. What ideas and pieces of knowledge are missing from the students' list? Consider providing a more traditional formative assessment of student knowledge on the day following the Fishbowl lesson.

Differentiation Ideas

To differentiate this lesson for a group of advanced or struggling students, create the list of words yourself prior to class. Include advanced vocabulary and challenging concepts for your advanced learners and simpler words to describe and act out those same advanced concepts for students who need support. Include the "passing" rule mentioned previously.

This activity also works well in smaller groups, so it is possible to designate two or more groups and play simultaneous games with multiple fishbowls. You can determine whether heterogeneous or homogeneous groups are most appropriate for allowing everyone a chance to stretch their thinking appropriately.

Lesson 7

A Picture Is Worth a Thousand Words

Objective

Students will prepare and present a 30-second creative speech based on a surprising image and the ideas generated by others in the class.

Rationale

Are your students captivated by internet memes, AI-generated images, and visual surprises? Mine definitely are and this lesson gives them a chance to respond to images creatively while practicing higher-level thinking and public speaking skills. The magical part of this activity is actually in the missing information. The images should be mentally stimulating with

 DOI: 10.4324/9781003657163-9

Figure 7.1 A Picture Is Worth a Thousand Words Classroom Setup

multiple aspects to analyze and evaluate. They are the kind of pictures or short videos that you might use for a "Notice and Wonder" activity. However, the remaining mystery of how and why the image exists should not be officially revealed and instead spark the need for someone to explain, synthesize, and create.

It is important to emphasize that this lesson is all about making inferences as well as divergent and creative thinking. This means there is not one correct answer or perfect 30-second explanation speech. As long as teams can justify their thinking by referring back to parts of the image, they may wonder about and imagine all kinds of potential scenarios that may have created it. This type of thinking is important for bright middle school students who have often been trained to limit their thinking to please teachers and correctly select multiple-choice answers on exams. Curiosity and divergent thinking will serve them well in solving the complex 21st century problems in their future when they will also need skills to collaborate and communicate with others (Thornhill-Miller et al., 2023).

Standards

NAGC 1.3. Self-Understanding. Students with gifts and talents demonstrate understanding of and respect for similarities and differences between themselves and their cognitive and chronological peer groups and others in the general population.

NAGC 4.2. Social Competence. Students with gifts and talents develop social competence manifested in positive peer relationships and social interactions.

NAGC 4.5. Communication Competence. Students with gifts and talents develop competence in interpersonal and technical communication skills. They demonstrate advanced oral and written skills and creative expression.

Preparation

Lesson Duration: 20–60 minutes

Materials Required: At least one surprising or mysterious image or short video (see **Resource 7.1 A Picture is Worth a Thousand Words** for some example images), caption optional; 1 note card for each student group

Background and Setup 5–10 minutes: Select one or more mysterious images or short videos from the internet or create them with AI tools. Incorporate concepts from your curriculum along with pop culture and other visual items of interest to your students.

Step-by-step Facilitation

1. Divide the class into partners or groups of three.
2. Show the image or short video on the board and ask students to examine it silently for at least 30 seconds.
3. Students may raise hands to ask questions or share specific things they notice in the image. It is important not to answer questions at this time. Focus on questions that ask why or how something came to exist in a certain way.
4. After questions have died down, pass out one note card to each pair of students.
5. Students have five minutes to create a 30-second speech that can answer one of the why or how questions asked by the class about the image. They may not conduct

any outside research, but should use their imaginations as much as possible while still referring to specific information present in the image. They should note bullet points of their speech on the note card, elect a speaker, and practice giving a persuasive and entertaining presentation.

6. After the five minutes are up, take volunteers to present the speech. The first group to present has the easiest task, because they do not have to incorporate any details except what they already planned and what is visible in the image.
7. The class should applaud after the speech and take a few minutes to note any changes they want to make to their own speeches.
8. A second group now sends a speaker up to present. This group must include at least one point made by the previous speaker along with the explanation they were already planning. They should state whether they agree or disagree with claims made by the previous speaker, referring back to evidence in the image.
9. Continue giving speeches until each group has sent a speaker to answer a question about the image while either agreeing or disagreeing with a previous group.
10. Repeat with a new intriguing image.
11. Close this lesson with an exit ticket asking students to rate their creative ideas and/or public speaking skills on a scale from 1 to 5 then provide at least 2 sentences of examples justifying their score.

Tips for a Successful Lesson

- **Finding or creating intriguing images**

  A simple Google search for "Intriguing Photographs" can provide a treasure trove of resources for this lesson. You may also browse the excellent video collections at https://thekidshouldseethis.com/. Include a search term referencing your curriculum to narrow the image search to your specific content. If you choose a real photograph or video that has not been digitally altered, it is important to cite your source including the photographer's name if possible. When using a real photo, I also spend a few moments after the class speeches answering as much as I can about the real origin of the photo. Alternatively, you can use Adobe, Canva, or other creativity tools to create or generate your own intriguing images. Try combining images or concepts from your curriculum with visual references to pop culture, internet memes, sports figures, or even your own classroom or students (with their permission). These custom images often spark the most creative and impassioned speeches from my classes! However, they also require a debrief about the responsibility to use AI generators and other visual tools with caution because of their tendency to mislead or misinform.

- **Speaking with Confidence**

  In this lesson, we are primarily assessing the creative inferences made by students with respect to the image presented. However, they all need practice with public speaking skills such as eye contact, clarity of message, and audience awareness. This exercise can help them improve each of these and especially their ability to speak with confidence. If you decide to use this lesson to practice or assess communication or presentation skills, I highly suggest selecting only one skill at a time and assessing it on a simple rubric along with the inferencing and creative thinking.

- **Academic Discourse**

  When students listen closely to each other's claims and choose whether to support with further evidence or suggest a counterclaim, they are engaging in academic discourse. Many middle school learners have not had direct instruction or practice with these skills and will need your guidance on how to agree or disagree respectfully. Even for a creative and open-ended activity like this one, students can learn to restate claims and provide further evidence or to use new evidence to respectfully disagree. Try providing sentence stems on the board prior to the speeches if you'd like to emphasize these skills more explicitly.

Assessment and Closure

The objective of this lesson is to prepare a creative speech that incorporates and responds to an intriguing image. Students should submit an exit ticket with a self-evaluation of their own creative thinking skills (and if appropriate their public speaking skills). As the instructor, you may keep this information as a formative measure. Alternatively, during the next class period, you can offer a more in-depth formative assessment targeting students' understanding of the photos as they relate to your curriculum content.

Differentiation Ideas

Flexible grouping is an appropriate strategy for differentiating this lesson. Your most advanced students should be grouped together and required to present last. They will have the greatest challenge of presenting something new and unusual while incorporating all ideas from the previous groups.

Another way to differentiate this lesson is to provide a set of sentence starters for ELL students or groups who are struggling to get started. These should be developed by you and related specifically to the image. For example, "The man on the far right of the image is thinking . . ." or "The photographer was finally able to ________________ right after snapping this photo". This can help students overcome the analytical challenges of a complex image and get right to the creative thinking. If you have these prepared ahead of time on note cards, you can easily hand them to certain groups while others receive a blank card.

Part II

Charms To Channel Curiosity in Ten to Twenty Minutes

"Next Tuesday is Halloween!" Mia reminds me as she announces she'll be coming to school dressed as a supreme court justice. I can't believe this holiday falls on a weekday again! I'm feeling a bit overwhelmed. We survived the first quarter but next week is also fall parent-teacher conferences. I wonder if I can plan something curious and exciting for Tuesday's class to harness that special middle school energy that comes on a day full of disguises, pranks, and candy. All my classes are beginning to trust each other at this point in the year, but I'd really like to incorporate a way for them to work together and practice some communication skills while introducing the second quarter's new unit. I'm especially hopeful that Kyla will speak up and the others will listen to her good ideas. What kind of lesson can make all that possible?

Of course, Halloween is only one energetic day of the year. I'm sure you can think of others – Valentine's Day, April 1st, the entire month of May. The next section of this book contains seven magical lessons that will jump-start your students' thinking and harness their natural enthusiasm even on the most unusual days. Each of these activities can be prepared in about ten to twenty minutes of planning time. You may need to dig up some unusual items or make a few copies to create these moments of magic, but it will pay off big time when you experience deep thinking from your students, imaginative ideas, and joyful social interactions. No technology is necessary for these experiences so it doesn't matter if their one-to-one devices aren't charged. Customize any of these lessons to your current content and enjoy the sparks of magical middle school energy they create in your classroom.

 DOI: 10.4324/9781003657163-10

Lesson 8

Human Knot

Objective

Students will demonstrate cooperative problem-solving skills and recognize each other's strengths.

Rationale

This magical lesson is a great way to build teamwork through movement and problem-solving. When you set this up correctly, your students physically become both the problem and the solution! If you haven't already tried this as an active participant during an adult training or team-building day, I highly encourage you to gather a few friends or family members and try it for yourself. You'll quickly see how the experience is both incredibly challenging, mysterious, and rewarding.

 DOI: 10.4324/9781003657163-11

The Human Knot is usually done by asking participants to physically hold each other's hands, but anyone who has ever taught middle school knows this would never work out well in a classroom full of young adolescents. Most of us don't even like doing this with other adults! So, several years ago I decided to adapt it by using small sturdy cloth bands as connecting links, rather than requiring my students to actually touch each other. This has effectively turned the shouts of, "Eew, no way!" into "Wow, that was fun, can we try it again?"

You can expand this lesson into a complex investigation of mathematical knot theory or just use it as a highly engaging problem-solving challenge that will bring your classroom joy and connection. However, I do not recommend trying this on the first day of class or even during the first week of school. It takes some established trust, because when they first create the knot, it will seem impossible to solve. One of the hallmarks of an effective gifted classroom is that it should be a safe place to be curious and take risks (Galbraith & Delisle, 2015). This activity will require both and it teaches students to persevere through some initial confusion and multiple failures. It will also have the entire room laughing and cheering together in that perfectly wonderful way that lets you know something magical is happening.

Standards

NAGC 3.5. Instructional Strategies. Students with gifts and talents become independent investigators.

NAGC 4.2. Social Competence. Students with gifts and talents develop social competence manifested in positive peer relationships and social interactions.

Preparation

Lesson Duration: 20–30 minutes

Materials Required: Fabric loops approximately six inches in diameter.

Background and Setup 10–15 minutes: Obtain or make a class set of sturdy fabric loops.

Step-by-step Facilitation

1. Divide students into groups of five to eight. Each group should form a circle.
2. Distribute one fabric loop to each student and instruct them to hold it in their RIGHT hand.
3. Students place their RIGHT hand with the loop into the center of the circle.
4. Then each person should reach into the circle with their LEFT hand and grab a loop that does not belong to them. Once they grab that loop, they are free to adjust their grip, but should not let go.
5. Allow time for the group to untangle themselves. They will need to twist, climb over and under each other's arms, and sometimes spin around with their hands above their heads.
6. If someone releases their loop and the connection breaks, the whole group must start again. Expect multiple failed attempts and praise them for learning what "doesn't work".
7. While the groups are untangling themselves, you should provide encouragement but try not to coach unless a group is completely stuck.
8. After the group is finished, they should have one large circle or sometimes two interlocked circles.
9. Debrief as a class to identify which strategies were the most helpful. Remind the class to continue reflecting on strategies because this will be their exit ticket.
10. Repeat the human knot with increasingly larger groups until you have completed it with the entire class of students working together.

Tips for a Successful Lesson

- **Loops that Work**

  I highly recommend creating your own reusable loops from sturdy recycled cotton or linen. Cloth napkins work well when cut into strips and tied securely. You can also sew the ends together if you are handy with a sewing machine. Do not attempt to use elastic bands because they can tighten or snap and hurt your students' hands when twisted and stretched.

- **Not Your Neighbor**

  If students are thinking carefully, they will quickly realize the knot is much easier to solve if they just grab the loop of the person standing next to them in the initial circle. To avoid this, try requiring that they grab a loop from anyone who is "not your neighbor". You can also try adding the rule that two people cannot both be holding each other's loops, which creates a tiny circle of only two people.

- **Coaching from Above**

  Your natural classroom leaders (or students reluctant to get close to others) can become a "coach" by giving instructions from outside the knot. If you feel it is safe, standing on a nearby chair can really help the coach visualize the knot problem more clearly and provides some physical movement for them as well. If you do not have an assigned coach, you can stand somewhere above the knot to provide help if the group gets stuck.

- **Unsolvable?**

  It is possible – but rare – for a group to accidentally create a real knot that cannot be untangled into a perfect circle, no matter what moves they use. In this case, you can congratulate the group on their correct use of knot theory and spend a few minutes exploring why this might happen. In this fascinating but obscure branch of mathematics, all knots are closed loops exactly like the ones created by the human knot activity. Your students will likely enjoy the Sci Show introduction to knot theory, or they can try using knotplot.com for various examples of mathematical knots. You can also introduce the terms "Unknot" and "Reidemeister Move" for explaining why the human knot can almost always be untangled with the right set of actions. The classic Trefoil and Figure 8 knots are great for beginners to see types of knots that cannot be untangled.

Assessment and Closure

Exit ticket on note card or Post-It. Which strategy was most effective for solving the knot quickly even with a large group?

Differentiation Ideas

Support struggling students by acting as the "coach" during the first round. Increase the difficulty by making the group larger or by adding a countdown timer. Expand this lesson into solving other knot problems or by adding a hands-on exploration of knots made with yarn.

Figure 8.1 Trefoil Knot

Lesson 9

Cards and Categories

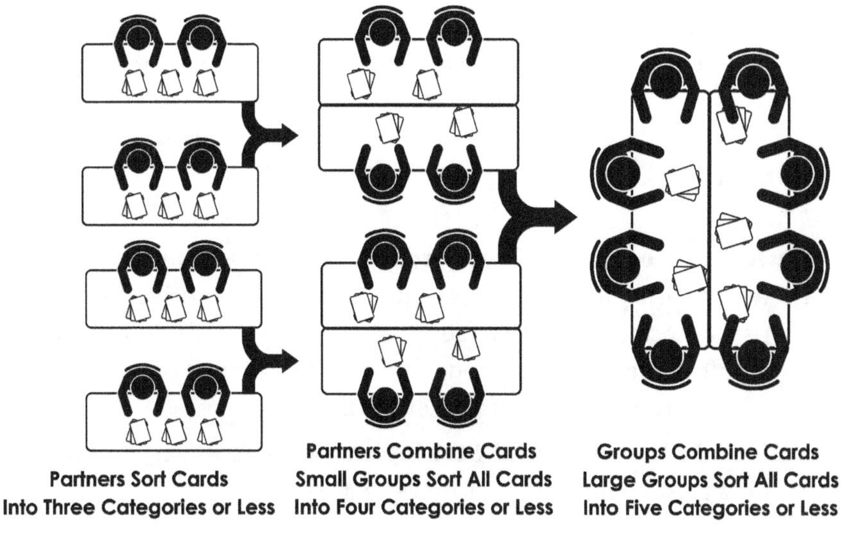

Figure 9.1 Cards and Categories Workflow Diagram

DOI: 10.4324/9781003657163-12

Objective

Students will categorize terms or concepts and justify their reasoning to peers.

Rationale

This lesson requires high levels of critical thinking while slowly increasing the challenge of group communication and collaboration. Students have the opportunity to think analytically and creatively as they manipulate objects in space and justify their placement to peers. They also move around the room while coming to a low-stakes group consensus. When the sorting is complete, they practice summarizing and critiquing the final group decision as they compare it to their own original thinking. For example, the history card set at the end of this chapter containing concepts about World War I could be sorted into many generic categories such as people, places, and things or into categories based on Central or Allied powers. At the end of the sorting, individual students may reject all of these categories and decide that groupings based on chronological periods of the war make the most sense and defend that analysis in an oral or written response.

This lesson incorporates some very important middle school interpersonal skills and can be easily customized to any curriculum content. It is another magical antidote to individual review activities such as flashcards, worksheets, and online games because it requires students to understand and defend the conceptual connections between many different types of facts, symbols, and ideas. It also prepares them to write a well-constructed essay over a complex topic or to give a well-organized oral presentation.

Standards

NAGC 1.5. Cognitive, Psychosocial, and Affective Growth. Students with gifts and talents demonstrate cognitive growth and psychosocial skills that support their talent development as a result of meaningful and challenging learning activities that address their unique characteristics and needs.

NAGC 3.5. Instructional Strategies. Students with gifts and talents become independent investigators.

NAGC 4.2. Social Competence. Students with gifts and talents develop social competence manifested in positive peer relationships and social interactions.

Preparation

Lesson Duration: 20–60 minutes

Materials Required: 25–50 cards with images, terms, or concepts from the current unit of study

Background and Setup 10–20 minutes: Create the set of cards by printing images on cardstock or writing terms neatly on three by five note cards. Alternatively, ask students to create the cards, but beware of duplicates and important concepts they may forget to include. Before class, conduct your own personal sorting of the entire deck into five categories or fewer to anticipate student thinking. Remove any unnecessarily difficult cards but stay open to new and creative categorization possibilities.

Step-by-step Facilitation

1. Group students into partners.
2. Distribute an equal number of cards to each pair of students.
3. Ask partners to sort their cards together into exactly three named categories. They must be able to name the category and justify why each card belongs there (categories cannot be based on letters or spelling). Emphasize that there are many possible correct ways to sort the cards.
4. Move throughout the room, helping students as needed. Remind them to think conceptually and creatively to connect ideas in expected and unexpected ways.
5. Call on each pair to name their three categories for the class, giving examples.
6. Join partners into small groups of four or six students. Partners should bring their original set of cards.
7. Ask the newly formed small groups to combine all their cards and sort again to four named categories. They may repeat earlier

categories if these continue to fit the new cards, or they may create new categories.

8. Call on each small group to name their four categories for the class, giving examples.
9. Continue increasing the group size and repeat until the entire class becomes the final group sorting the entire deck of cards.
10. Ask the class to determine five or fewer named categories that all the cards could fit into.
11. After the final decisions are made, each individual student critiques the final category selections along with their own original categories.

Tips for a Successful Lesson

- **Silence is Not Golden but Timing is Key**

  Expect students to make noise during this lesson that is primarily focused on oral communication! Encouraging them to share their ideas out loud also means they may not always stay on topic. I have found that active listening and strategic use of a countdown timer can keep discussions productive and minimize tangents. Start by listening, then asking simple questions to each pair or group as you walk through the room. When you notice that over half the groups are completely finished or have gotten off topic, set a timer for one minute for remaining groups to finalize their categories.

- **Disagreeing Politely**

  This activity requires students to repeatedly fit new ideas into their existing frameworks and to engage in productive academic discourse with peers. Beware that these skills do not come easily to many gifted middle school students! Especially if you have not already taught a lesson on academic discourse, I suggest quickly reviewing how to disagree politely with someone and ways that a group can come to a fair decision even when not all members agree. It may even be a good idea to list helpful and unhelpful phrases on the board. Pay close attention to the group dynamics as you walk around the room and gently guide conversations only when needed. If you decide to provide communication suggestions that would benefit the entire class, do so between rounds without singling anyone out.

- **Addressing Misconceptions**

  Interestingly, disagreements may arise from genuine misconceptions or misinformation even in a class of gifted students who seem confident in their grasp of the terms or ideas on the cards. As these arise, first listen and let students try to reach an accurate conclusion on their own. Then, if necessary, lean into these teachable moments and provide explanations, even looking something up quickly if needed. I find it helpful to document any nuanced details that I provide during the discussion by jotting them down on the back of the card(s) in question. This way students can refer back to my notes in later rounds and I have a record for myself of which cards caused some confusion.

Assessment and Closure

Students should be able to define and justify their own personal categorizing system, giving examples for each group. They may agree or disagree with the final group system, and their answers may be written or oral.

Differentiation Ideas

Add more variety to cards and/or increase the number of total cards to increase the difficulty. Increase the thinking challenge by using symbolic graphics or photos rather than terms. You may also consider adding a time limit or disallowing the use of "Miscellaneous" as a category name.

To provide support, include captions, definitions, or examples on the back of the cards as needed, especially for advanced or unfamiliar concepts. Consider assigning certain cards to students who will have the most success with these concepts initially or consider assigning partners and groups strategically. Another way to provide support during frequent disagreements is to allow the use of subcategories. Subcategories do not count toward the maximum number allowed in the round, but can allow students to tease out small differences that they believe are important.

Example Set of Cards Reviewing Concepts From World War I (created with help from generative AI and verified with reputable sources)

Archduke Franz Ferdinand	Assassinated on June 28, 1914, in Sarajevo, his murder triggered the chain reaction leading to World War I. As heir to the Austro-Hungarian throne, his death provided the immediate pretext for war. Britannica
Trench Warfare	Dominant from 1914–1918, especially on the Western Front, where soldiers lived in long, static dugouts. Its stalemates, mud, and high casualties defined the brutal trench conditions of WWI. Imperial War Museums
Allied Powers	Comprised Britain, France, Russia, and later the U.S. and Italy between 1914–1918, united against the Central Powers. Their combined military and economic strength contributed to their ultimate victory. History.com
Central Powers	Germany, Austria-Hungary, the Ottoman Empire, and Bulgaria formed this alliance. They were defeated in 1918, resulting in significant postwar territorial and political shifts. BBC Bitesize
Western Front	Stretching through France and Belgium, this front saw trench warfare from 1914–1918. Major battles like the Somme and Verdun occurred here, with heavy casualties but little territorial change. National WWI Museum
Eastern Front	Spanning the Baltic to the Black Sea, it was more mobile than the Western Front. Intense fighting occurred from 1914–1917 until Russia's withdrawal following revolution. British Library
Battle of the Somme	From July–November 1916, it resulted in over 1 million casualties, symbolizing WWI's futility. The offensive aimed to relieve French pressure at Verdun but resulted in limited gains. Imperial War Museums
Battle of Verdun	Spanning February–December 1916, Verdun was one of the longest and bloodiest battles in history. The French mounted a determined defense against a major German offensive. History.com
Lusitania	A British passenger liner, sunk by a German U-boat on May 7, 1915, killing 1,198 people including 128 Americans. The event helped shift U.S. public opinion toward entering the war. Naval History & Heritage Command
Zimmermann Telegram	Sent in January 1917, it proposed a German-Mexican alliance if the U.S. entered the war. Its interception galvanized American support for joining the conflict. National Archives
No-man's-land	The deadly area between opposing trenches, often covered in mines and corpses. Crossing this zone during offensives led to severe losses. History.com

Barbed Wire	Widely used from 1914–1918 to fortify trenches and slow enemy advances. It became a symbol of WWI trench warfare's deadly barriers. Imperial War Museums
Machine Gun	Capable of firing hundreds of rounds per minute, it transformed battlefield tactics by making infantry charges deadly. Its widespread deployment in 1914 brought unprecedented lethality. History.com
Poison Gas	First used on a large scale in 1915, gases like chlorine and mustard inflicted severe injuries and psychological terror. The horror of gas warfare prompted the development of gas masks and later bans. Imperial War Museums
Tanks	Debuted at the Battle of the Somme in 1916, tanks were designed to cross trenches and break stalemates. Though unreliable initially, they marked the dawn of armored warfare. Imperial War Museums
Airplanes	Used initially for reconnaissance in 1914, they evolved into fighters and bombers during WWI. Dogfights and aerial raids became key components of modern warfare. Imperial War Museums
U-boats	German submarines used stealth attacks to disrupt Allied maritime supply lines. Their success in sinking civilian and military vessels escalated the war at sea. History.com
Unrestricted Submarine Warfare	Reinstituted by Germany in February 1917, allowing attacks on all ships near Britain. This policy provoked U.S. entry into WWI by targeting civilian shipping. History.com
Total War	WWI saw full mobilization of society – economies, industries, and civilians – between 1914–1918. This comprehensive approach included rationing, conscription, and wartime production. BBC Bitesize
Propaganda	Governments used posters, films, and speeches to boost recruitment, demonize opponents, and sustain morale during long stalemates (1914–1918). Propaganda became a central tool in shaping public opinion. Imperial War Museums
Selective Service Act (U.S.)	Enacted in May 1917, this act authorized drafting American men into the military. By war's end, over 2.8 million U.S. soldiers were conscripted. U.S. Army Center of Military History
Russian Revolution	Revolutions in March and November 1917 overthrew the Tsar and led to Bolshevik control. British Library
Woodrow Wilson	U.S. president during WWI, serving from 1913–1921, he guided the U.S. into war in April 1917 and championed the idea of a League of Nations. Wilson Center
Kaiser Wilhelm II	German Emperor from 1888–1918, his militaristic policies and support of Austria-Hungary helped precipitate the war. Facing imminent defeat, he abdicated in November 1918, ending the German monarchy. Britannica
Treaty of Versailles	Signed on June 28, 1919, this treaty formally ended WWI and imposed reparations and territorial losses on Germany. The treaty's punitive measures fueled resentment and helped lay the groundwork for WWII. National Archives

Fourteen Points	Announced by Wilson in January 1918, these principles advocated self-determination, open diplomacy, and the League of Nations. They influenced the postwar settlement, though not all were fully incorporated. U.S. State Dept
League of Nations	Founded in 1919 to promote peace and resolve disputes diplomatically. Without U.S. participation, the League lacked authority and ultimately failed to prevent WWII. League of Nations Archives
War Guilt Clause	Article 231 of the Treaty of Versailles in 1919 formally blamed Germany for WWI. This clause served as justification for reparations and was a major source of German resentment. National Archives
Reparations	Germany was required to pay reparations totaling 132 billion gold marks after 1919. The financial burden devastated Germany during the Weimar Republic years. U.S. Holocaust Memorial Museum
Armistice (Nov. 11, 1918)	Signed at 11 a.m. on November 11, 1918, this agreement ended combat on the Western Front. The date is commemorated as Armistice Day or Remembrance Day. Imperial War Museums
Ottoman Empire	Allied with the Central Powers from 1914–1918, it suffered massive territorial losses and eventual collapse. Its demise led to the founding of modern Turkey in 1923. British Library
Gallipoli Campaign	From 1915–1916, Allied forces attempted to seize the Dardanelles and open a supply route to Russia. The campaign failed, bolstering Ottoman defense and influencing national identities in Australia and Turkey. Australian War Memorial
Battle of Tannenberg	In August 1914, German forces decisively routed Russia in East Prussia. The victory elevated Commanders Hindenburg and Ludendorff in German military hierarchy. German History Docs
Italian Front	A series of mountain battles from 1915–1918 between Italy and Austria-Hungary. The harsh Alpine terrain and conditions made it a uniquely brutal theater of war. International Encyclopedia of the First World War
Red Baron (von Richthofen)	Manfred von Richthofen scored 80 aerial victories before being killed in April 1918. As Germany's top fighter pilot, he became an icon of air combat. Imperial War Museums
Alvin York	American soldier who, in October 1918, led an attack capturing 132 German soldiers, earning the Medal of Honor. He became one of the most famous U.S. heroes of the war. U.S. Army Center of Military History
Mobilization	Rapid troop and resource deployment in 1914 ignited the war when various nations prepared for large-scale conflict. Mobilization schedules and treaties turned a regional crisis into a global war. History.com
Conscription	Mandatory military service used by major powers, ensuring large armies for a prolonged conflict. Its widespread use from 1914–1918 reflected the total war paradigm. BBC Bitesize
Spanish Flu (1918–1919)	Pandemic that struck during the end of WWI and killed an estimated 50 million worldwide. It crippled armies and civilian populations, compounding the war's devastation. CDC
Lost Generation	Refers to the generation disillusioned by WWI's horrors, captured in literature by authors like Hemingway and Fitzgerald. The term reflects the deep social and cultural impact of the war. Encyclopedia Britannica

Example Set of Cards Reviewing Landforms

(created with help from generative AI and verified with reputable sources)

Plate Tectonics	A unifying theory explaining the movement of Earth's lithospheric plates, which causes earthquakes, volcanic activity, and mountain formation. Plate tectonics is the driving force behind many surface landforms. USGS
Continental Drift	Proposed by Alfred Wegener, this early 20th-century hypothesis suggested continents move slowly over Earth's surface. It set the stage for modern plate tectonics. Britannica
Mountain Range	A series of mountains connected by high ground, often formed by the collision of tectonic plates. Notable ranges include the Himalayas and the Rockies. NPS
Volcano	A landform created by the eruption of magma from beneath the Earth's crust, forming features like cones, islands, and calderas. Volcanoes can build land and dramatically alter landscapes. USGS
Fault Line	A fracture in Earth's crust where tectonic plates meet and slide past one another, often causing earthquakes. The San Andreas Fault is a famous example. USGS
Earthquake	The sudden shaking of the ground caused by movement along a fault line. Earthquakes can reshape land and lead to the formation of new surface features. USGS
Fold	A bend in rock layers formed by compressional forces deep in Earth's crust. Folds can form hills and mountain ridges over time. Britannica
Valley	A low area between hills or mountains, typically formed by river erosion or glacial activity. Valleys may be V-shaped (river) or U-shaped (glacial). National Geographic
Glacier	A large mass of moving ice that carves out land as it flows. Glaciers create landforms like U-shaped valleys, moraines, and fjords. NPS
Delta	A fan-shaped deposit of sediment at a river's mouth where it meets a body of water. Deltas are fertile and often densely populated. National Geographic
Canyon	A deep, narrow valley with steep sides, usually carved by river erosion over millions of years. The Grand Canyon is one of the most famous examples. NPS
Mesa	A flat-topped hill with steep sides, formed by erosion in arid environments. Mesas are common in the American Southwest. Britannica
Butte	A smaller version of a mesa, standing isolated with steep sides and a flattop. It forms through prolonged erosion. Britannica
Arch	A natural rock formation shaped like an arch, typically formed by wind or water erosion. Arches are common in desert regions like Utah. NPS
Spit	A narrow landform made of sand or gravel extending from the coast into a body of water. Spits form through longshore drift. Britannica
Barrier Island	Long, narrow islands running parallel to the mainland, protecting coastlines from waves and storms. These dynamic landforms shift frequently. NOAA
Sand Dune	A hill or ridge of sand shaped by wind, found in deserts and coastal areas. Dunes migrate over time due to wind patterns. NPS

Beach	A landform along the shoreline composed of loose particles like sand or gravel. Beaches constantly change due to tides, waves, and human activity. NPS
Erosion	The process by which water, wind, or ice removes and transports soil and rock. Erosion shapes many landforms and can cause environmental challenges. NPS
Deposition	The process by which sediments are laid down in new locations, creating features like deltas and sandbars. It works hand in hand with erosion. Britannica
Weathering	The breakdown of rocks and minerals into smaller particles by physical, chemical, or biological means. It is the first step in soil formation. USGS
U-Shaped Valley	A glacially carved valley with a rounded, U-shaped cross-section. These valleys show where glaciers once flowed. NPS
V-Shaped Valley	A valley carved by a river, featuring a narrow bottom and steep walls. Common in youthful river systems. Britannica
Drumlin	A smooth, teardrop-shaped hill formed beneath glacial ice. It indicates the direction of glacier movement. Britannica
Moraine	A ridge or mound of debris deposited by a glacier. Moraines mark the former edge of glacial movement. Britannica
Alluvial Fan	A fan-shaped deposit of sediment formed where a stream slows down abruptly. Found at the base of mountains in arid areas. Britannica
Sinkhole	A depression caused by the collapse of a surface layer, often in regions with limestone bedrock. Sinkholes can occur suddenly and be very dangerous. USGS
Karst Topography	A landscape shaped by the dissolution of soluble rock such as limestone, featuring caves, sinkholes, and underground rivers. Common in Florida and parts of China. NPS
Tombolo	A sandbar or spit that connects an island to the mainland or another island. Formed by wave refraction and sediment deposition. Britannica
Island Arc	A curved chain of volcanic islands formed at a subduction zone where an oceanic plate sinks beneath another. Japan and the Aleutians are examples. Britannica

Lesson 10

Trivia Buzzers

Objective

Students will recall factual information and build cooperation skills by analyzing questions as a team.

Rationale

Answering factual questions correctly and quickly is a natural skill for many gifted learners. Forced recall is also a highly effective memory technique that can reinforce learning (Soderstrom et al., 2016). This lesson broadens a typical trivia session by creating a space for personal knowledge to shine while intentionally rewarding collaborative recall and listening skills. It is always a favorite with my classes because we have

DOI: 10.4324/9781003657163-13

customized rules that are fair for both extroverts and introverts as well as quick thinkers and deep thinkers.

The highlight of this lesson for most students is the use of handheld individual response devices. The buzzers provide an instantaneous and equitable way to determine who knew the answer first! The excitement of pressing the button, hearing the tone, and watching for the instant recognition light is similar to the dopamine rush of a video game but can be applied in real time to questions selected by the teacher while also requiring the interpersonal skills of effective oral communication, turn-taking, and teamwork.

The following procedure highlights a balance between individual brilliance – "I knew that answer first!" – and team collaboration – "We discussed the question and got the best answer when we took our time!" The key to making this work is to immediately follow any incorrect buzzer answers with a longer opportunity for all teams to discuss the difficult question and then rotate the opportunity to "steal" the points by providing a team answer for double or even triple the number of points. This discourages random guessing and encourages students to collaborate and learn from each other. They also must listen closely to each answer to avoid repeating an incorrect guess.

Standards

NAGC 1.3. Self-Understanding. Students with gifts and talents demonstrate understanding of and respect for similarities and differences between themselves and their peer group and others in the general population.

NAGC 4.5 Communication Competence. Educators ensure access to advanced communication tools, including assistive technologies, and use of these tools for expressing higher-level thinking and creative productivity.

Preparation

Lesson Duration: 20–60 minutes

Materials Required: Electronic response devices (scholar bowl or similar), Set of customized questions, Timer, Dry-erase Board (or other place to keep score).

Background and Setup 10–15 minutes: Select a list of factual questions applicable to current learning or standard curriculum at least one grade level above. You will need to prepare at least five questions per minute, depending on difficulty. If assessing cooperation skills, make sure students have access to the rubric you will be using. Prepare a slide with your customized rules or list them on the board before class.

Step-by-step Facilitation

1. Form teams of three to five students each.
2. Distribute buzzers to each student or pair of students.
3. Review rules for any individual or team-based scoring including a potential Quiz Out Rule (see **Resource 10.1 Rules and Tips for Trivia Buzzers!** for a customizable example).
4. Test buzzers so everyone confirms they have an equal chance to answer.
5. Start timer, read questions, and track points for individual correct responses.
6. When the first response given is incorrect, allow an opposing team to discuss the question for at least 30 seconds before answering for a doubled number of points. If this team is incorrect, allow another team a chance to answer for triple the points (when teams earn double or triple points I award these to the individual team members with the least number of points on the board).
7. If no one is able to correctly answer the question, pause the timer to quickly explain the correct answer and warn students you will likely bring that question back again later. Then restart the timer and move to a new question.
8. If one or two students are dominating the buzzers, institute a Quiz Out Rule (see forthcoming).
9. End questions when time is up and total points by team.

Tips for a Successful Lesson

- **Obtain High-Quality Buzzers**

  "Buzzers" or personal response devices are available in many different styles and often used for state- and nationally sanctioned competitions such as Scholar Bowl and Quiz Bowl. Many schools may already have a set of buzzers to use in these competitions and these team sponsors often welcome collaboration with a teacher who can encourage future participation from bright learners. If you need to purchase a set of your own buzzers, there are many factors to consider before you invest. They need clear lighting, sounds, a consistent power source, and the ability to quickly and accurately reset. Carefully read reviews by other teachers to determine what will best meet the needs of your classroom environment.

- **Encouraging Timely Collaboration**

  Students will quickly figure out that buzzing in early just to guess randomly allows the other teams to dominate through collaboration and steals. They may try to discuss prior to pressing the buzzer and/or confirm with a teammate after buzzing in. You can determine how strictly to enforce the rule that collaboration can occur only after an incorrect answer is given. This will depend on whether your goal is to review as many questions as quickly and accurately as possible or if your priority is to encourage cooperation and teamwork.

- **Customize the Quiz Out Rule**

  Before each timed round of questions, set a limit on the number of questions that can be answered correctly by one individual student. Once a student has reached that number, they are "Quizzed Out". In my class, this means they get a round of applause from the room, a bonus point, and get to go sit on the couch for the remainder of the round. We want to provide recognition for their amazing knowledge but also give time and space for others to answer. I choose the number of points required to quiz out based on many factors, including the length of the round, how comfortable my students are with the content, and the size of each team. In a ten-minute round with three students per team, five points is usually a good baseline quiz out number.

- **Accidents**

  Determine how you will handle "accidental" buzzing before you start the round. I allow one accident per person. Students will claim they didn't mean to hit the buzzer and yes, this really happens. After the second accident, I start to subtract points from the overexcited buzzer and this helps keep things under control.

- **Good Sportsmanship**

  Take this opportunity to clearly teach some important life skills related to competition. Clearly explain that "trash talk" is not allowed. They will get excited and want to cheer when their team gets an answer correct. This should absolutely be encouraged!

However, it is never okay for students to berate each other for making a mistake. If necessary, rehearse an appropriate response that can express disappointment in a wrong answer but also be encouraging at the same time.

Assessment and Closure

Total points earned by each team. Assess team-based skills on customized cooperation rubric if desired.

Differentiation Ideas

To extend the challenge, write questions that require higher-level thinking. To provide support, use technology to make questions visual as well as auditory. Utilize a flexible response system to improve control over who can respond to each question.

Table 10.1 – Teamwork Rubric for Eighth Grade Gifted Trivia

Criteria	Exceeds Expectations (3)	Meets Expectations (2)	Needs Improvement (1)
Participation	Actively participates in all trivia questions, offering ideas and solutions. Encourages and supports all team members to contribute.	Participates in most trivia questions, occasionally offering ideas. Tries to include all team members.	Rarely participates or offers ideas during trivia questions. Does not actively engage with the team.
Communication	Communicates ideas clearly and respectfully. Listens attentively to teammates and values their input. Helps resolve any conflicts or disagreements.	Communicates ideas adequately. Listens to teammates but does not always incorporate their suggestions. Tries to resolve minor conflicts.	Has difficulty communicating ideas or listening to teammates. Does not contribute to resolving conflicts within the team.
Cooperation	Consistently works well with the team, sharing responsibilities and supporting each other. Demonstrates flexibility and a positive attitude.	Usually works well with the team, but may occasionally struggle to share responsibilities or support teammates.	Has difficulty cooperating with the team, often unwilling to share responsibilities or support teammates. Displays a negative attitude.

Example Question List for Middle School Trivia

Category	Question	Answer
ELA	What is the singular form of the word "fungi"?	fungus
Miscellaneous	In what month do we observe Martin Luther King Day?	January
History	What do we call the group of department heads who aid the U.S. President?	the Cabinet
Science	What branch of science studies elements, atomic theory, and compounds?	chemistry
Math	Give the sum of these fractions as a mixed number: 7/8 + 3/8	1 and 2/8 or 1 and 1/4
Geography	Name three countries that are islands	Japan, Australia, New Zealand, Cuba, etc.
ELA	What does it mean to "debug" a computer program?	to remove malfunctions (called bugs)
Miscellaneous	In what game do you hear the words "check" and "stalemate"?	chess
History	America is named for what explorer?	Amerigo Vespucci
Science	What gas is represented by the letters "He"?	Helium
Math	"Radius" and "diameter" are associated with what geometric figure?	circle
Geography	Which continent has the warmest climate?	Africa
ELA	Say the contractions for the words "cannot", "will not", and "do not".	can't, won't, don't,
Miscellaneous	Who created Sherlock Holmes?	Sir Arthur Conan Doyle
History	What river did the Native Americans call "the father of the rivers"?	Mississippi
Science	When does a solar cell give off electricity?	when it is hit by sunlight
Math	Name four prime numbers	2, 3, 5, 7, 11, 13, 17, 19, etc
Geography	What language do most of the people speak in Ottawa, Johannesburg, and Sydney?	English
ELA	What form of the pronoun "who" is used as a direct object?	whom
Miscellaneous	On a sheet of music, how many lines does each staff have?	five
History	Which leader of the former Soviet Union won the Nobel Peace Prize in 1990?	Mikhail Gorbachev

Science	What system in the human body is destroyed by the disease called AIDS?	immune system
Math	If a book that costs $25 is marked up by 5%, what is the final price?	$26.25
Geography	In what country will you find the Gobi Desert?	Mongolia
ELA	Use one prefix to form antonyms of all these words: enchanted, honest, advantage.	disenchanted, dishonest, disadvantage
Miscellaneous	What are chilies and jalapenos?	peppers
History	Which New England colony was the first to outlaw slavery in 1777?	Vermont
Science	Why, in outer space, does a spacecraft keep moving on its own?	There's significantly less gravity or friction to slow it down.
Math	Add eight feet, six inches to nine feet, nine inches. What's the sum?	18 feet, 3 inches
Geography	What do we call the indigenous peoples of Australia?	Aborigines
ELA	Is *The Last of the Mohicans* fiction or nonfiction?	fiction
Miscellaneous	Translate the Latin expression "Tempus fugit"	Time flies
History	What imaginary line once separated free states from slave states?	the Mason-Dixon line
Science	In what organ of the human body does a stroke occur?	the brain
Math	How many acute angles does an acute triangle contain?	three
Geography	Which hemisphere contains the Tropic of Cancer?	Northern Hemisphere
ELA	You can lead a horse to water, but you can't make him . . . what?	drink
Miscellaneous	In what country does the Olympic flame begin its trip to the site of the Games?	Greece
History	A historic battle was fought at the Alamo. In what city and state is the Alamo?	San Antonio, Texas
Science	How many watts do you use in one kilowatt-hour?	1,000 watts
Math	A segment that joins two points on a circle is called . . . what?	a chord
Geography	On what continent are the cities of Bangkok and Shanghai?	Asia
ELA	Add a prefix to "circle" to form a word that means "half a circle".	semi- (semicircle)

Miscellaneous	In what city can you watch a sports event at Madison Square Garden?	New York City
History	What is the only country ever to use the atomic bomb as a weapon?	the United States
Science	Why do water pipes sometimes burst in extremely cold weather?	The water inside them expands when it freezes.
Math	What metric unit measures the liquid in a large bottle of water?	liters
Geography	What happens to temperatures as altitude increases?	temperatures decrease
ELA	Reverse two letters in the word "angle" to find a heavenly being.	angel
Miscellaneous	What vitamin is added to milk because it helps us absorb calcium?	vitamin D
History	In 2009, Barack Obama appointed what woman as U.S. Secretary of State?	Hillary Clinton
Science	What color does litmus paper turn if you drop acid on it?	red
Math	Each corsage has two roses and three violets. How many flowers are in 12 corsages?	60
Geography	The islands of Bali and Java are part of what large country?	Indonesia
ELA	Spell the simple past tense of "omit".	o-m-i-t-t-e-d
Miscellaneous	What U.S. state hosts the dogsled race called the Iditarod?	Alaska
History	Who was president when congress passed the Civil Rights Act of 1964?	Lyndon B. Johnson
Science	Why does water in a pot begin to move when you heat it?	because hot water rises from the bottom
Math	What is the reciprocal of 9 and 2/3?	3/29
Geography	What language do the natives of Athens speak?	Greek

Lesson 11

One of These Things Doesn't Belong

Objective

Students will analyze a set of four mystery objects to determine which one does not belong with the others and justify their reasoning to persuade peers.

Rationale

This lesson involves a lot of movement around the room while students also learn to think analytically and creatively in the style of Danielson's (2023) book *Which One Doesn't Belong? Playing With Shapes*. There is mystery created by hiding the physical objects and students mingle with each other by selecting where to stand each round. In this activity you are searching for

 DOI: 10.4324/9781003657163-14

Figure 11.1 One of These Things Doesn't Belong Classroom Setup

multiple correct answers and especially for divergent and unique answers. It can open the door to understanding multiple perspectives and solving problems in unique ways.

Students appreciate that this activity is fast-paced with music and they get to hold things in their hands while thinking! The cognitive skill of making connections between disparate objects is equally important to the skill of differentiating a unique characteristic that sets one object apart. These skills are useful in all kinds of academic analysis from literature to science experiments. My middle school gifted learners also love having the chance to point out a unique and detailed observation that someone else may have missed. This lesson offers the opportunity for social validation when peers agree with a creative idea and physically move closer to the person who came up with it.

Standards

NAGC 1.3. Self-Understanding. Students with gifts and talents demonstrate understanding of and respect for similarities and differences between themselves and their cognitive and chronological peer groups and others in the general population.

NAGC 4.2. Social Competence. Students with gifts and talents develop social competence manifested in positive peer relationships and social interactions.

NAGC 4.5. Communication Competence. Students with gifts and talents develop competence in interpersonal and technical communication skills. They demonstrate advanced oral and written skills and creative expression.

Preparation

Lesson Duration: 20–60 minutes

Materials Required: Four similar opaque boxes with lids, at least four sets of related but different objects, 30-second song to play while students move around the room, spinner or sticks with student names to call on people randomly.

Background and Setup 10–15 minutes: Gather sets of four related but different objects to hide in the boxes. Use hands-on manipulatives from your curriculum, or see the example lists at the end of this chapter. Place the first set of objects into the boxes and arrange them on four different desks in four corners of the room before class starts. Place slides with instructions on the board and cue up your 30-second theme song (see **Resource 11.1 One of These Things is NOT Like the Others** for a customizable example).

Step-by-step Facilitation

1. Review the rules with students seated and the first four items hidden inside four boxes around the room. Provide multiple examples and answer any questions about the procedure.
2. Ask the entire class to stand, push in chairs, and stow backpacks so everyone can move as freely as possible around the room.
3. Start the theme music and allow students to move around to peek at each object.
4. When the music stops, each student should stand next to the box containing the object that they believe doesn't belong with the others.
5. Spin a wheel of names or draw name sticks to randomly select a student. That person should share their choice and justify their answer. I ask students to justify in three parts.
   In this example the four items are a pencil, a pen, a highlighter, and a paintbrush.
   a. State the category that all four objects belong to.
      Example: All four of these are used for making art.
   b. State what three of the objects have in common.
      Example: Three of them are made of plastic.
   c. State what makes your selected object different from the other three.

Example: The pencil is made from wood.

6. Next draw another name and allow that student to share their choice and justification. Continue until all the objects that have at least one person next to them have been defended.
7. To complete the round, all students whose names were not drawn should move to the box with the student who they think had the most creative and accurate reasoning.
8. Ask students to bring the boxes to your desk where you will replace the items with four new mystery objects.
9. Repeat steps 3–7 with all the sets of items.
10. Close with students ranking their own thinking on a rubric.

Tips for a Successful Lesson

- **Swapping Items in the Boxes**

  You will need a way to swap items into the boxes quickly and secretly to maintain the fast pace and mystery of this lesson. If you have at least eight boxes available, you can facilitate a quicker turnaround by packing two sets of boxes before class. Then during the second round while students are moving around, you can replace the items from the first round with objects for the third round.

- **Keeping Score**

  There is an option to make this activity more competitive by having students keep their own score. I assign one point to everyone whose name is drawn and defends an answer correctly. They also get additional points for anyone else who ends the round at their table and agrees their answer is best. You can decide if keeping score in this way is motivating to your students or will cause them undue anxiety.

Assessment and Closure

Provide a creative thinking rubric (see appendix) for each student to rate their own thinking during the lesson. Conduct your own assessment during the lesson using a roster of your students' names and noting an E for each time you hear them share an *expected* connection and C for each time you hear them share a *creative* connection. Use this data to determine which students need more opportunities to think creatively about connections between objects and ideas.

Differentiation Ideas

This lesson naturally offers a low floor and a high ceiling, meaning that students can successfully participate even with relatively shallow thinking skills. However, the deepest and most creative thinkers will automatically see the opportunities to go beyond the expected. To further support all students, you can provide multiple examples prior to starting the activity or provide a longer time for students to move around and think about their choices.

If you feel your advanced students are ready for a greater challenge, try incorporating a fifth optional item in a box in the center of the room. If students choose to use it, the item must be included in every group and cannot be the one that doesn't belong. This extension really stretches thinking. You can also take advanced students' thinking deeper by using objects or images that often symbolize other big ideas. Try this set of four objects for a deep thinking challenge and a rich discussion of ideas: an American flag, a wooden cross, a white bird, and a plastic skull.

Example Groups of Mystery Objects

The following groups of objects can promote interesting connections and are easily found in a home or middle school setting.

Group 1	Group 2	Group 3	Group 4	Group 5	Group 6
Apple	Golf Ball	Scissors	Calculator	Bag of Hot Chips	Pencil
Tangerine	Whiffle Ball	Glue	Navigational Compass	Candy Bar	Candle
Banana	Balloon	Sharpie	Watch	Can of Soda	Battery
Avocado	Egg	Ruler	Phone	Pack of Gum	Match

Lesson 12

Mystery Guest

Objective

Students will use deductive reasoning to correctly identify the name of a mystery character or historical figure.

Rationale

This magical lesson brings my middle school classes so much joy because they love having a secret that everyone else in the class is trying to figure out! Our stated goal is usually to review the nuanced differences between various characters or historical figures, but importantly students also hone their questioning skills. They all get a few moments in the spotlight to answer the questions, but spend more time thinking

 DOI: 10.4324/9781003657163-15

Figure 12.1 Mystery Guest Classroom Setup

of relevant questions that will get the entire group closer to solving the mystery. Students who want to can highlight their improvisational performance skills, while quieter students and introverts often solve the mystery with their superior listening skills.

The role-playing aspect of this lesson also teaches important social communication skills such as turn-taking and active listening. Using a handheld prop microphone that magnifies voices only slightly helps students refrain from talking over each other and only speak when they are holding the mic. Through this type of practice, they learn to interact with peers in respectful and positive ways to develop the advanced communication skills required for academic discourse and future leadership roles.

Standards

NAGC 3.5. Instructional Strategies. Students with gifts and talents become independent investigators.

NAGC 4.2. Social Competence. Students with gifts and talents develop social competence manifested in positive peer relationships and social interactions.

NAGC 4.5. Communication Competence. Students with gifts and talents develop competence in interpersonal and technical communication skills. They demonstrate advanced oral and written skills and creative expression.

Preparation

Lesson Duration: 20–60 minutes

Materials Required: Class set of cards with names and descriptions of the mystery guests (optional: microphone prop, comfortable seating, and theme music).

Background and Setup 10–20 minutes: Prepare cards with names of each potential mystery guest including any necessary background information, dates, or descriptions. Select theme music to play when guests enter and exit the stage. Arrange chairs at the front of the classroom to mimic a talk show set.

Step-by-step Facilitation

1. Distribute mystery guest cards to each student, reminding them to keep their identities secret. Allow time for students to review any information on the cards and privately ask you questions if needed.
2. Review rules for Mystery Guest on a slide (see **Resource 12.1 Mystery Guest Rules** Slide).
3. The teacher is the first "HOST" and asks for a volunteer to be the first mystery guest.
4. Start theme music briefly then mute it as you welcome everyone to the mystery guest show and review today's theme. (Students should applaud enthusiastically whenever the theme music plays and sit quietly when it is not playing. Practice this if necessary.) If you want your hosts to riff for a bit with the audience before sitting in the host chair, demonstrate this with a smile and hint at a few questions you can't wait to ask today's guest.
5. The mystery guest should go out to the hallway and then enter when they hear the welcome music start up again. Audience applauds during the music and guest entrance. The host should stand to welcome the mystery guest with a handshake or fist bump.
6. Mystery guest and host sit when the music fades and the applause ends.
7. Host thanks the guest and asks the first question to get the conversation started (see upcoming tips for examples of polite questions that can be asked.)

8. Guest answers each question with a short comment or quick story but does not give away too much.
9. Host calls on any audience members with their hands raised and brings them the microphone to ask questions to the mystery guest, who answers. Alternately, you can pass around an audience microphone.
10. When anyone is ready to guess the mystery guest's name they must be called on by the host and ask, "Is your name ___________?"
11. If they are correct, they become the next mystery guest and the current guest becomes the new host.
12. Repeat steps 5–10 until everyone has had a chance to be the mystery guest. If a student guesses the correct name but has already had a turn, they should nominate another student to be the next guest.
13. Close this lesson by asking students to evaluate their questioning skills on a rubric.

Tips for a Successful Lesson

- **Polite Questions Only**

  Questions about the guest's accomplishments, family life, place of residence, etc. are all fair and "polite" questions that can provide clues and get the guest to tell some interesting stories. Questions about the guest's physical appearance, race, or gender are not allowed because they would be impolite to ask anyone sitting directly in front of you. As the teacher, you have the responsibility of warning any hosts or audience members who ask impolite questions and guiding them to a more appropriate query.

- **Lean into the Performance**

  You may encourage students to lean into the performance of their character by doing vocal impressions or imitating the mannerisms of the person they are portraying. Some students will love to take this acting as far as possible while others will prefer to keep it simple and use their own natural voice. Either way is fine because the emphasis should be on the questions and answers.

- **Improvisation versus Reality**

  Sometimes students may get carried away when impersonating a character and decide to invent stories or events as the mystery guest that are not technically true. They may also make mistakes in remembering the facts. Your job is to listen closely to all guest responses and evaluate them for credibility. Before starting the show, let students know that as the teacher, you reserve the right to raise your hand and ask questions that will carefully clear up any misunderstandings and if you need to help, you will do so without giving too much away.

Assessment and Closure

This lesson is a fun and exciting way to review and compare different characters or historical figures, but it is also a practical way to hone questioning skills and deductive thinking. Close the lesson by asking students to reflect on their questioning skills on a rubric. Follow this up in the next class period with another more formal assessment of your content-based objectives.

Differentiation Ideas

To differentiate this lesson quickly, plan ahead to assign certain characters to specific students. All the cards should appear the same and it should not be obvious that they are at different levels. Advanced students need to receive more complex or obscure guests that require a more in-depth knowledge of the material. Struggling students or those with less background knowledge should be assigned character cards with more additional details provided.

Another differentiation option is to provide sample question stems on the backs of the character cards. These can be used by audience members and hosts during the show or used ahead of time for students to prepare for the types of questions they may be asked. Adjust the final questioning rubric appropriately if you are using question stems.

Finally, this lesson can be naturally differentiated, by allowing students to select their own mystery guest character in a prior class period and conduct background research. This also gives them time to bring props or costumes for the next class period if desired. If you are using this option, spin a wheel or otherwise select students randomly to approach your desk and select their character from a list. You can provide suggestions and track who each student selects. You will need to help students keep their research secret, but can also provide additional support this way to any students who need it.

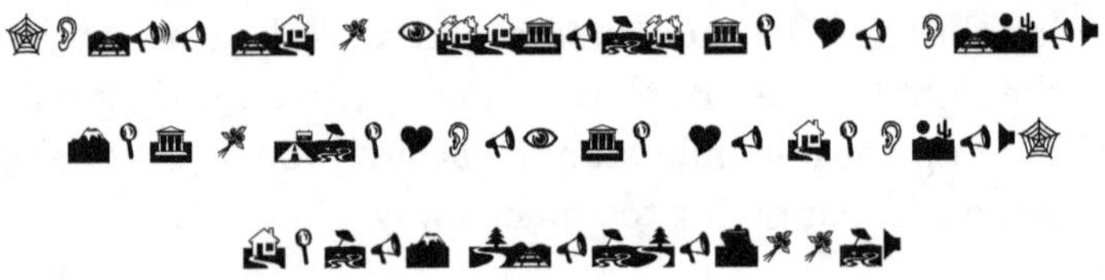

Example Lists of Mystery Guests

Mystery Guests from *The Outsiders* (Hinton, 1967)	World War II Mystery Guests	Mystery Guest Scientists
Ponyboy Curtis	Winston Churchill – Prime Minister of the United Kingdom; led Britain through WWII with powerful speeches and steadfast resistance to Nazi Germany.	Albert Einstein (1879–1955) – German-born theoretical physicist; developed the theory of relativity, revolutionizing modern physics.
Darry Curtis	Eleanor Roosevelt – First Lady of the U.S.; advocate for human rights and support for troops and civilians during the war.	Marie Curie (1867–1934) – Polish-born physicist and chemist; pioneered research on radioactivity and was the first woman to win a Nobel Prize.
Sodapop Curtis	Franklin D. Roosevelt – President of the United States; guided the U.S. through the Great Depression and most of WWII until his death in 1945.	Isaac Newton (1643–1727) – English mathematician and physicist; formulated the laws of motion and universal gravitation.
Cherry Valance	Nancy Wake – Member of the French Resistance and British Special Operations Executive (SOE); known as The White Mouse for her stealth.	Galileo Galilei (1564–1642) – Italian astronomer and physicist; improved the telescope and supported heliocentrism, challenging traditional views of the cosmos.
Dally Winston	Joseph Stalin – Leader of the Soviet Union; key Allied leader whose forces played a major role in defeating Nazi Germany on the Eastern Front.	Rosalind Franklin (1920–1958) – British chemist; produced key X-ray images that led to the discovery of DNA's double helix structure.
Johnny Cade	Sophie Scholl – German student and anti-Nazi activist; executed for distributing anti-Hitler pamphlets with the White Rose movement.	Charles Darwin (1809–1882) – English naturalist; proposed the theory of evolution by natural selection through his work *On the Origin of Species.*
Two-Bit Mathews	Dwight D. Eisenhower – Supreme Commander of Allied Forces in Europe; led the D-Day invasion and later became U.S. President.	Gregor Mendel (1822–1884) – Austrian monk and biologist; known as the father of genetics for his experiments with pea plants.
Steve Randle	Virginia Hall – American spy for the SOE and OSS; operated behind enemy lines despite having a prosthetic leg, nicknamed the Limping Lady.	Thomas Edison (1847–1931) – American inventor; held over 1,000 patents including the phonograph and the electric light bulb.
Sandy	Adolf Hitler – Dictator of Nazi Germany; initiated the war with the invasion of Poland and orchestrated the Holocaust.	Nikola Tesla (1856–1943) – Serbian-American inventor; known for his work on alternating current (AC) electricity systems.
Marcia	Lyudmila Pavlichenko – Soviet sniper credited with 309 kills; one of the most successful female snipers in history.	Katherine Johnson (1918–2020) – African-American mathematician; calculated critical NASA flight trajectories, including for Apollo 11.

Mystery Guests from *The Outsiders* (Hinton, 1967)	World War II Mystery Guests	Mystery Guest Scientists
Randy Adderson	Benito Mussolini – Fascist leader of Italy and Hitler's ally; overthrown in 1943 and executed in 1945.	Stephen Hawking (1942–2018) – British theoretical physicist; made key contributions to black hole physics and the nature of the universe.
Bob Sheldon	Clare Hollingworth – British journalist who broke the story of Germany's invasion of Poland in 1939.	Ada Lovelace (1815–1852) – English mathematician; considered the first computer programmer for her work on Babbage's Analytical Engine.
Tim Shepard	Charles de Gaulle – Leader of the Free French Forces; later became President of France and symbol of resistance.	Louis Pasteur (1822–1895) – French chemist and microbiologist; developed pasteurization and vaccines for diseases like rabies and anthrax.
Curly Shepard	Josephine Baker – African American entertainer who smuggled messages for the French Resistance using invisible ink on sheet music.	Benjamin Franklin (1706–1790) – American polymath; experimented with electricity and invented the lightning rod and bifocals.
Mr. Syme	Erwin Rommel – German general known as the Desert Fox; respected for his tactics in North Africa, later implicated in anti-Hitler plot.	Rachel Carson (1907–1964) – American marine biologist and author of "Silent Spring"; sparked the modern environmental movement.
S. E. Hinton	Rosie the Riveter – Symbolized American women working in factories and shipyards during WWII; represented a major shift in gender roles.	Alexander Fleming (1881–1955) – Scottish biologist and pharmacologist; discovered penicillin, the world's first true antibiotic.
Buck Merrill	Emperor Hirohito – Emperor of Japan during WWII; symbolically led the country during its military expansion and eventual surrender.	Jane Goodall (1934–) – British primatologist; transformed our understanding of chimpanzees and promoted animal conservation.
Jerry Wood	Hannah Szenes – Jewish paratrooper from British Mandate Palestine; captured and executed after parachuting into Europe to aid resistance.	Carl Sagan (1934–1996) – American astronomer and science communicator; popularized science through the TV series *Cosmos*.
	George S. Patton – U.S. general noted for his leadership in North Africa, Sicily, and across Europe after D-Day.	Barbara McClintock (1902–1992) – American geneticist; discovered transposable elements (jumping genes) in corn and won the Nobel Prize.
	Vera Atkins – British intelligence officer with the SOE; responsible for placing female agents in occupied France and investigating their fates post-war.	George Washington Carver (c. 1864–1943) – African-American agricultural scientist; promoted crop rotation and alternative crops to improve farming.

Lesson 13

Memory Display

Objective

Students will apply memory strategies to remember as many items or words as possible.

Rationale

Do you love to watch students push themselves to do their best and improve their personal levels of focus, concentration, and working memory? This magical lesson reinforces all these skills while engaging everyone in a fast-paced hands-on activity. It also has the motivating bonus of peer-created mystery. Half of your learners will be moving around the room selecting the most interesting combination of objects and terms for their peers to

 DOI: 10.4324/9781003657163-16

memorize while you work with a smaller group to teach thinking strategies right when they are highly motivated to listen and immediately apply them.

If you have already created a custom deck of cards for Lesson 9 to review images, terms, and concepts for your current unit of study, these cards can be incorporated into the memory trays for additional discussion and review. This means even less prep time for you and more joyful and rigorous learning for your students!

Standards

NAGC 1.5. Cognitive, Psychosocial, and Affective Growth. Students with gifts and talents demonstrate cognitive growth and psychosocial skills that support their talent development as a result of meaningful and challenging learning activities that address their unique characteristics and needs.

NAGC 3.5. Instructional Strategies. Students with gifts and talents become independent investigators.

NAGC 4.2. Social Competence. Students with gifts and talents develop social competence manifested in positive peer relationships and social interactions.

Preparation

Lesson Duration: 45–60 minutes

Materials Required: timer, cloth napkins or small opaque tablecloths, note cards, books, or various items from around the classroom, paper and pencils, plastic lunch trays to hold objects (optional)

Background and Setup 10–15 minutes: Determine which memory strategies your students need to learn and prepare a short explanation with examples. Provide plenty of small objects, books, printed images, or cards for students to browse around the room. Prepare one example desk of 12 items and cover it with a colorful cloth so students will notice it immediately upon entering the classroom.

Step-by-step Facilitation

1. Ask the class to guess how many items are under the cloth and if they have any ideas what the items might be.

2. Explain that they will have one minute to memorize everything they can see on the desk once you remove the cloth, then one minute to write a list of all the items.
3. Start your timer and remove the cloth.
4. Replace the cloth after exactly one minute.
5. Make sure all students have paper and pencils ready, then start the timer to list all the items they can remember.
6. After one minute, announce pencils down and remove the cloth again.
7. Discuss the number they got correct as their "baseline" score and let them know today they will all learn a strategy to help remember more things quickly.
8. Divide the class into pairs.
9. One partner from each pair will go to a back section of the room or into the hallway with the teacher to learn a memorization strategy.
10. The other partner selects 12 different small objects, books, images, and/or cards for their partner to memorize. These objects should be carefully arranged on a desk so each is clearly visible and separate, then the entire desk should be covered with a cloth.
11. In the hallway or in a back corner of the classroom, share the memorization strategy and examples of how to use it with one set of students.
12. When all tables have been arranged with 12 items and covered, students from the hallway may rejoin their partners in class.
13. Start the timer for one minute of memorization with the tables uncovered and then for one minute of listing with the items covered.
14. Return all items to their original location in the classroom.
15. Swap roles and repeat.

Tips for a Successful Lesson

- **Selecting an Effective Memory Technique to Teach**

  Not all memory strategies will work for all students equally so take some time to review the research and select one that you believe will be most helpful for your particular group. I find that the *Memory Palace*, also known as Plato's Loci technique (McCabe,

2015), is effective and fun for creative students with great imaginations (for example, students may imagine walking past each of the items in rooms of their house, clearly visualizing each item in a memorable place). My classes have also enjoyed the *Create A Song* technique, especially when they can quickly apply a tune they already know such as the tune to "Twinkle, Twinkle, Little Star". You also may want to try *Mnemonics*, *Chunking*, or the *Storytelling* techniques. Descriptions of various memory techniques can be found at https://learningcenter.unc.edu/tips-and-tools/enhancing-your-memory/ Each time you teach this lesson, you can provide your students with a new tool that may work for them.

- **Keep It Organized**

  When students are allowed to select any objects from around the room, they get very creative, and this is part of what makes this lesson so exciting. However, this creativity can quickly become a nightmare for you if you don't plan ahead for cleanup time. Each student's selected object or card must be returned to its original location by the tray creator as described in step 14. If you will not have much time for reorganizing the items before the end of class, you can try adding a rule that items must come from students' own backpacks or from one designated table of objects that you are personally willing to put away at the end of the day.

- **Try It Yourself First**

  Ask a teacher friend or family member to select and cover 12 items for you to memorize in one minute. Establish your own baseline score before attempting to use a memory technique yourself and try a few different ones. Sharing your baseline and progress with students can help them understand that this lesson is valuable and not just a gimmick.

Made-to-order Mystery

This lesson can be customized to any content you are studying if you have many hands-on manipulatives available or if you create a deck of cards with images or terms. I sometimes make my initial baseline tray according to a theme based on our curriculum, so they can see an example of how to do this. However, the completely random item selection makes the memory challenge more exciting and is quicker to prepare.

Assessment and Closure

Debrief by discussing the following questions: Did the memorization strategy help improve your score? Which types of items were easier to remember and why? How could you apply these memory skills when studying for a test, meeting a new group of people, or witnessing an important event?

As an exit ticket, each student should record their growth in the number of items remembered and a reflection on whether the strategy was helpful or not.

Differentiation Ideas

To increase rigor, require all selected items to fit a specific theme or category. You may also increase the difficulty by increasing the number of items or reducing the amount of time. To provide support, reduce the number of items, or increase the amount of time.

If students are interested in learning more about the psychology of memory and learning, you can stretch this lesson into an entire problem-based inquiry by posing the question, "What is the best way to learn something that you want to remember forever?" There are several excellent

Figure 13.1 Example Mathematics Memory Display

TED Talks available on memory, and gifted students often enjoy learning about neural anatomy and how to train their brains. Neuroscience for Kids is another treasure trove of resources, experiments, and kid-friendly brain research. The human brain itself is a complex hidden mystery that many gifted middle school students find fascinating.

Resource 13.1 Exit Ticket Example:

Name ______________________ Class Period ________

Score 1 Baseline ___________

(Number of items I memorized on the teacher's memory display)

Memory Technique I learned ____________________________

Score 2 After applying technique __________

Difference between Score 1 and Score 2 ___________

Is the memory technique helpful? Why or why not?

____

____

Lesson 14

Musical Madness

Figure 14.1 Musical Madness Setup

DOI: 10.4324/9781003657163-17

Objective

Students will accurately answer a series of challenging questions while building social competence and problem-solving skills.

Rationale

This lesson is similar to the birthday party classic game, musical chairs. However, students must correctly answer a question in order to keep their seat! It was born from a need to get my students away from their devices and physically moving and socializing while practicing important curricular concepts and higher-level thinking. In the years following the COVID pandemic, I began observing other middle school classes and examining my own lessons closely. I started to realize students were spending almost all day at school looking at screens rather than each other or the physical world around them. I know there are many incredible benefits to the use of technology and I certainly don't want to remove it altogether as an educational tool for my learners. However, this lesson (and many of the others in this book) suggest ways that we can take digital guided practice and turn it into social guided practice with numerous developmentally appropriate benefits for our young adolescents.

Musical Madness also capitalizes on the excitement and surprise of suddenly hearing your favorite song while moving your entire body and getting blood flowing to your brain (Ferreri et al., 2019). Music is one of the easiest avenues to explore positive differences in cultural background and learn to appreciate every student's unique artistic interests and influences (Davis, 2005). Each time a song is played and paused during this lesson, someone gets to claim it and judge the round while others answer a difficult question. If you are ready to get students up and moving, thinking, and interacting, this lesson will definitely bring magic to your middle school classroom.

Standards

NAGC 1.3. Self-Understanding. Students with gifts and talents demonstrate understanding of and respect for similarities and differences between themselves and their cognitive and chronological peer groups and others in the general population.

NAGC 4.2. Social Competence. Students with gifts and talents develop social competence manifested in positive peer relationships and social interactions.

Preparation

Lesson Duration: 30–45 minutes

Materials Required: Chairs, Question Cards, Class Playlist, Dry-erase Boards, Markers and Erasers

Background and Setup 10–15 minutes: Place at least two question cards face down on each chair in a circle of chairs facing the outer walls of the room. Make sure there is one fewer chair than the total number of students. Cue up your class playlist on shuffle. Place two dry-erase boards with markers and erasers near the chairs and distribute the other boards at desks where eliminated players will eventually sit.

Step-by-step Facilitation

1. Allow each student to choose a seat in the circle directly on top of the question cards (one student will remain standing.)
2. Review the rules and answer any questions.
3. Start the first song on your shuffled playlist and let it play for approximately 30 seconds while students walk around the chairs in a single file line in the same direction.
4. Stop the song and watch students quickly choose a seat. Whoever is left without a seat gets to choose who they want to challenge. They should stand next to that person who must also stand up, vacating the disputed seat.
5. Whoever recommended the song that was just playing becomes the judge (unless they are part of the challenge, then the teacher is the judge). The judge selects a question card from the empty seat and hands each challenger a dry-erase board and marker.
6. The judge reads the question, giving the challengers a few moments to think and write their answers.
7. Next the judge picks the most complete and accurate answer or declares a tie and picks another question. The student with the incorrect or least accurate answer is eliminated.

8. The eliminated student gets to choose which chair to remove during the next song, redistributing its cards. Eliminated students may return to the game by playing along during each new challenge. They can be called on by the judge if neither challenger is correct.
9. Repeat steps 3–8 with a new song each time until all the chairs but one are eliminated.
10. Close the lesson by asking students to complete an exit ticket answering the most difficult question of the lesson.

Tips for a Successful Lesson

- **Creating the Playlist**

  This lesson can be done with a teacher-created playlist and a randomly selected judge using a spinner or name sticks. However, I have found that it is much more magical when the class chooses the music. In fact, you may have noticed that many of the lessons in this book incorporate music somehow. Middle school students are often excited to share their burgeoning musical interests with you and with their peers. It is an incredibly important part of their personal culture and identity that is easy to celebrate. At the beginning of the school year, you can ask students to name their favorite artist and school-appropriate song. Then put together the class playlist with clean versions of the songs on your favorite streaming platform. I recommend always playing it on shuffle, so you don't get blamed for giving preference to any one person's song. If you don't want the distraction of lyrics, many popular songs are available on YouTube in karaoke or instrumental versions. This playlist will come in handy for independent work time as well as lessons like "Musical Madness".

- **Card Shuffling Option**

  If you have a large question set and want to keep things exciting, you can ask students to "shuffle" the question cards while they walk around. This means they are allowed to pick up one card only and move it to another chair as they walk. In this way, they often review the cards quickly and tend to be more careful about where they choose to sit or challenge. Do not stop the music while students are holding cards.

- **Managing Mild Mayhem**

  Just like regular musical chairs, this review activity gets exciting and, especially toward the end, it can get physical. Decide up front how much physical contact or speedy walking you want to allow while keeping all your students safe. Make it very clear that anyone who breaks the safety rules will be automatically eliminated. I recommend demonstrating what is okay and not okay before the first round.

Assessment and Closure

After the final chair has been won or all the questions have been answered, allow students time to reflect on their knowledge and participation. Provide a note card or sticky note to each student to answer the question: What was the most difficult question asked today and what was the correct answer? As a teacher, complete your own reflection on students' knowledge by sorting the question cards as the lesson goes along. Sort the question cards into three piles: one pile for questions that ended in a tie for two correct answers; one pile for questions that one student clearly answered more accurately than another; and a third pile for questions that both challenger students answered incorrectly. Use the data from both of these assessments to determine if further review or teaching is needed for these concepts.

Differentiation Ideas

To increase the challenge and review more questions, allow eliminated players to challenge any player they choose once between every round of music. The judge can preside over any of these additional challenges. Incorporate Kaplan's (2017) depth and complexity icons into your question development to raise the level of thinking for all questions.

To provide support when students are struggling, allow a longer period of time for circling the chairs and include the shuffling rule, which allows students to preview the cards and choose a seat based on answers they know.

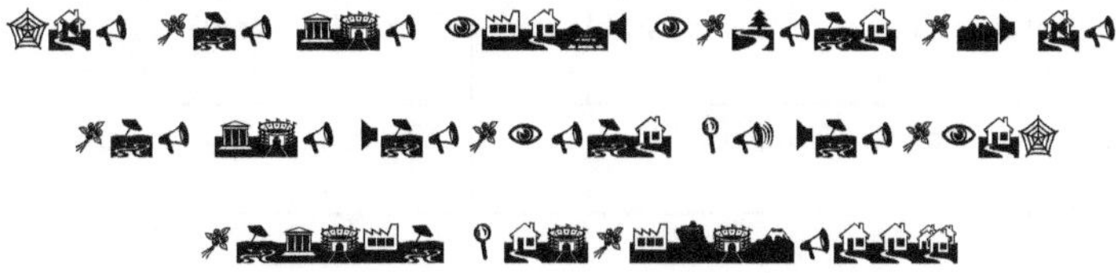

Resource 14.1 Example Physical Science Question Set for Musical Madness

Reviewing Properties of Atoms and the Periodic Table of Elements (Including Depth and Complexity Challenge Questions)

Question	Answer
Why are transition metals often used in building materials and electronics?	They are strong, conduct electricity, and form multiple oxidation states.
Using the icon of "Details", describe the specific characteristics of halogens.	Halogens are very reactive nonmetals in group 17, with 7 valence electrons.
What is the difference between an atom and an ion?	An atom has a neutral charge; an ion has a net positive or negative charge due to loss or gain of electrons.
Compare the number of valence electrons in carbon and neon. How does this affect their chemical reactivity?	Carbon has four valence electrons and readily forms bonds, while neon has eight and is chemically inert.
What causes the identity of an atom to change?	Changing the number of protons changes the identity of the atom.
Compare the atomic size of oxygen and fluorine. Which is smaller and why?	Fluorine is smaller because it has more protons, increasing nuclear pull on its electrons, even though it's in the same period.
What is the maximum number of electrons that can fit in the first energy level?	The first energy level can hold up to two electrons.
What is an isotope?	An atom of the same element with a different number of neutrons.
Explain the trend of electronegativity down a group.	Electronegativity decreases down a group as atomic size increases and electrons are farther from the nucleus.
Describe how electrons are arranged in an atom using energy levels.	Electrons are arranged in shells around the nucleus, with each shell holding a specific maximum number of electrons.
Why do elements bond with each other?	To achieve a full outer shell of electrons, becoming more stable.
What is a valence electron and why is it important?	A valence electron is in the outermost shell and determines how an atom bonds.
What is the significance of the "stair-step" line on the periodic table?	It separates metals from nonmetals and highlights the location of metalloids.
Which group contains elements that are stable and rarely react?	Group 18 - Noble Gases
What do elements in a period (row) have in common?	They have the same number of electron shells.

Compare sodium and chlorine in terms of their tendency to gain or lose electrons.	Sodium tends to lose one electron to form a cation, while chlorine tends to gain one electron to form an anion.
Using the icon of "Trends Over Time", how has the periodic table changed since Mendeleev's version?	It is now organized by atomic number instead of atomic mass and includes more elements.
Which element is the most electronegative?	Fluorine (F)
What is ionization energy and how does it trend across a period?	Ionization energy is the energy needed to remove an electron; it increases across a period.
Why is hydrogen placed separately on the periodic table?	It has one valence electron like group 1 but is a nonmetal with unique properties.
How do you calculate the number of neutrons in an atom?	Subtract the atomic number from the mass number.
Which group contains the most reactive metals?	Group 1 - Alkali Metals
What is the charge, location, and relative mass of a neutron?	Neutrons are neutral (no charge), located in the nucleus, and have a relative mass of 1 amu.
What is the difference between atomic mass and mass number?	Atomic mass is the average mass of all isotopes of an element; mass number is the total number of protons and neutrons in one atom.
What does the term "periodic" mean in the context of the periodic table?	Repeating or recurring patterns of properties across periods.
What do elements in the same group (column) of the periodic table have in common?	They have the same number of valence electrons and similar chemical properties.
Using the icon of "Patterns", what pattern do you notice about reactivity in alkali metals?	Reactivity increases as you move down the group.
Which element is in period 3, group 2?	Magnesium (Mg)
How do the number of protons in an atom relate to its atomic number?	The atomic number of an atom is equal to the number of protons in its nucleus.
Compare the reactivity of lithium and francium. Which is more reactive and why?	Francium is more reactive because it is farther down group 1, meaning its outer electron is more easily lost due to weaker nuclear attraction.
What is an anion and how is it formed?	A negatively charged ion forms when an atom gains one or more electrons.
Which two particles in an atom have equal but opposite charges?	Protons (positive) and electrons (negative) have equal but opposite charges.
Using the icon of "Ethics", should scientists create synthetic elements even if they are unstable? Explain.	Answers will vary; students may argue for or against, considering safety, knowledge, and purpose.
Which type of element is brittle and a poor conductor?	Nonmetals
What is a metalloid? Give two examples.	An element with properties of both metals and nonmetals; examples include silicon and boron.
Using the icon of "Rules", what are the basic rules for determining the number of valence electrons in a main group element?	For groups 1–2 and 13–18, the group number corresponds to the number of valence electrons.

Which type of element is typically malleable, ductile, and a good conductor?	Metals
Why are noble gases unreactive?	They have full outer electron shells.
Compare a metal like calcium to a nonmetal like sulfur in terms of physical properties.	Calcium is malleable, shiny, and a good conductor, while sulfur is brittle, dull, and a poor conductor.
What is a cation and how is it formed?	A positively charged ion formed when an atom loses one or more electrons.
Explain the trend of atomic radius across a period.	Atomic radius decreases across a period due to increasing nuclear charge pulling electrons closer.
What is the mass number of an atom?	The total number of protons and neutrons in an atom.

Part III

Developing a Deeper Mystery

More Than Twenty Minutes to Prep

It is almost too quiet in my classroom for a Friday morning. Today I have four blissfully uninterrupted contract hours to finalize grades and get set up for next quarter. As I finish scoring the last rubric, I glance around the room to decide which project most deserves this rare and special moment of professional freedom. I could rearrange my bulletin board. But the incredible posters Zai and Anthony designed really deserve to stay up a bit longer. I could reorganize my disastrous craft supplies shelf, but Evelyn has been asking to stay after school to help with that. Of course, there is always paperwork to be filed, emails to be sent, and the district-mandated training video I still need to watch. But none of these mundane tasks feels right. I'm caffeinated, creative, and I can play whatever music I want through my smartboard speakers for the rest of the morning. My eyes land on the closet where I have everything stored for next quarter and it seems to sparkle with a mysterious possibility. That's it! Today, I'm going to dig in to my next unit of curriculum and plan something new, something magical, and something that makes me as happy as my students.

The lessons in this final section are some of the most memorable hands-on experiences you can possibly create for your middle school gifted learners in only one class period. They do require more time to thoughtfully prepare but are so wonderful that students will come back years later still talking about them. The key to each of these activities is a customized and exciting mystery that ignites your students' natural curiosity and helps

 DOI: 10.4324/9781003657163-18

them sense the need to work together. Some of these lessons require special supplies and one requires a special guest, so you'll need to think ahead to make this magic happen. However, once you give it a try and watch your students come alive with curiosity and the joy of learning, you'll be determined to see that spark again.

Lesson 15

Codes and Ciphers

Objective

Students will apply problem-solving strategies to decode and encode secret phrases using various encryption techniques.

Rationale

This magical lesson builds thinking skills at the same time as classroom culture. The elements of surprise and mystery provide a natural motivation for students to engage in a highly difficult collaborative task – code-breaking. With a little made-to-order background preparation from their teacher, gifted students can understand, decipher, and create their own codes, which leads to a shared understanding of something mysterious, fun, and highly useful.

 DOI: 10.4324/9781003657163-19

Codes are at the foundation of the human desire to communicate and can be applied to almost any type of curriculum. Most teachers will realize that language, mathematics, music, and computer science all have their own unique symbols and codes. When students understand the patterns and rules of these codes, the more complex concepts of these disciplines can be unlocked. Codes and ciphers have also been used throughout history to communicate, protect, and preserve cultural societies. When you give your students a foundational lesson in codebreaking, you are handing them tools to apply throughout their future academic lives.

Years ago, I struggled with motivating my bright middle school students to analyze and decipher encrypted messages. Their brains were capable, but they often found the worksheets and exercises tedious, especially when assigned as independent practice. Even applying codes to programming video games was engaging only to a few. In order to inspire collective cognitive effort, I needed to find something mysterious and exciting enough that they would really want to know how to use a complex code immediately. This is where the celebrity guest comes in to make the magic possible. Their presence in the room and apparent ease with communicating to me through a code was naturally fascinating to my students, especially when they suspected the coded message was about them!

Standards:

NAGC 3.5. Instructional Strategies. Students with gifts and talents become independent investigators.

NAGC 4.5 Communication Competence. Educators ensure access to advanced communication tools, including assistive technologies, and use of these tools for expressing higher-level thinking and creative productivity.

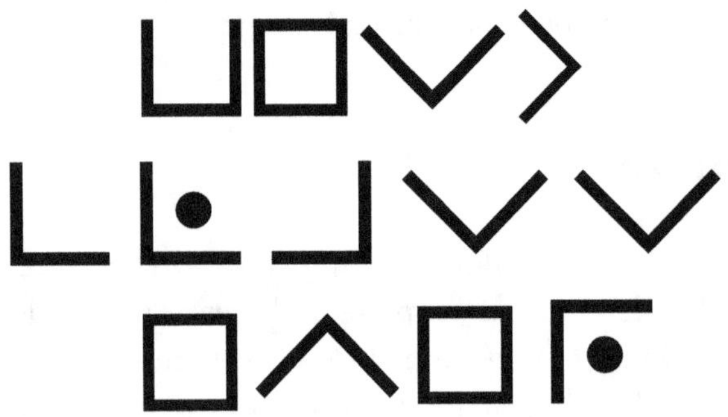

Figure 15.1 Pigpen Code Example Phrase

Preparation

Lesson Duration: 20–60 minutes

Materials Required: special celebrity guest, slides to introduce basic encryption techniques (see **Resource 15.1 Introduction to Codes and Cyphers** for a customizable example; make a copy and customize these to phrases your students will enjoy), dry-erase boards, dry-erase markers, erasers

Background and Setup 30–45 min: A few days prior to the lesson, invite a special celebrity guest (administrator, former teacher, custodial staff, neighbor teacher) to walk into your classroom at an agreed upon time and write a message in code somewhere obvious. Figure 15.1 provides an example message in pigpen code that my students found fascinating. Prepare practice encryption slides with messages customized to your students and using techniques your students do not yet know.

Step-by-step Facilitation

1. Distribute dry-erase boards, markers, and erasers to each student.
2. Use slides to introduce basic encryption techniques. Ask for students to make connections to codes they have seen in books, movies, or learned about at school.
3. Students should use the dry-erase boards to attempt to decode each message either before or after the cipher is revealed.
4. At the point that your special guest enters the room, students will notice them and hopefully pay attention to what they write.
5. After the guest leaves, someone will most likely ask you why they were in the room or ask something about the message. This is the point where you want to capitalize on the mystery.
6. Say something like, "Well, that is a pretty advanced code . . . do you want to try to crack it?"
7. Ask students to make connections between the code on the wall and the codes they have already learned. Look for patterns like repeated letters or breaks between words.
8. When students have cracked the special guest code with your help, allow time for them to write a message to your guest using the same code. You can deliver these to the guest a later time.
9. Then continue on with the slides and encryption techniques lesson.

Tips for a Successful Lesson

- **Supporting your Mystery Guest**

  Not all administrators or teacher friends will feel comfortable learning to communicate with you in code or acting as co-conspirators to surprise and mystify your students. Do your best to ask the right person at the right time. Explain the entire lesson and its ultimate purpose while also giving them a copy of the code. It is helpful to provide a sample message, and plan ahead for any special gestures. Let them know that you will be basically ignoring them as they write the message other than a quick nod indicating your understanding. If you have found the right mystery guest, they will also love to have a full recap of your students' reactions and the ultimate success of the lesson.

- **Valuing Productive Struggle**

  Many curious gifted students are uncomfortable not knowing something and can become frustrated when tasks are challenging. A key part of this lesson involves coaching them on how to work through these feelings, search out resources, and even ask others for help. Typical students experience productive struggle daily in general education, but gifted learners often miss the chance to develop grit and determination when classwork comes easily. Customize this lesson to the comfort level of your students by providing just enough support at the beginning and by giving hints on strategy when questions arise. You can also encourage them to work together. I often say something like, "I'm not sure I want you to know the code I use to communicate with the principal, but if you can figure it out together, I guess you all deserve to know". Resist the temptation to simply tell them the answer and your learners will thank you later.

Made-to-order Mystery

Customize this lesson by using personalized early examples as you are introducing simple ciphers and how to break them. I have had great results with brain rot slang, quotes from their favorite movies, and especially memes. You can also try starting with some vocabulary or phrases they might recognize from your curriculum or using your school mascot, motto, or a local athlete's recent accomplishments. Once they feel confident deciphering phrases they can recognize, they will be more confident attempting an unfamiliar message in a code they have not seen before.

Another wonderful made-to-order aspect of codes is the pure joy of secret communication. If you teach multiple groups of students like I do, having a unique cipher for each class or grade level can be a fun way to build community and even to differentiate. Allow students to help you develop the code or cipher and you will have permanent buy-in for any important future messages, but be sure to keep a copy of each key handy in a secure location. Codebreaking websites such as Cachesleuth (https://www.cachesleuth.com/multidecoder/) and Rumkin (https://rumkin.com/tools/cipher) are also readily available and easy to use, so it is also helpful to remember that nothing written in code is truly a secret.

Finally, in this lesson it is especially important to be aware of the unique needs of any twice exceptional students with dyslexia or any second language learners. For anyone who struggles with spelling, understanding a coded phrase can be extra challenging. However, these gifted students are often the best codebreakers, because they use this type of cognitive skill daily by looking at context clues, making inferences, and seeking overall meaning. This is why I recommend students **mingling** to work together and learn from each other's strengths.

Assessment and Closure

Assess accuracy of coded messages to your special guest or the messages students create for each other at the end of the lesson.

Differentiation Ideas

To level up this lesson, use more advanced codes. See the examples at the end of this chapter or the list of codes and descriptions at https://www.instructables.com/Best-Codes/. To support students, provide a printed copy of the alphabet with blanks underneath so they can fill in the substitutions and track them throughout the lesson.

Fun Codes, Ciphers, and Phrases for Middle School

Try a few of the following short coded phrases to get your middle school gifted students interested in codes and ciphers.

- What do you call it when Black Beauty signals for help?

  – –.-. . . . .. / -.-. – -. . .

- Hide a stash of prizes under a couch or armchair, then give students this riddle in the Gold Bug code invented by Edgar Allen Poe using typewriter keys.

  1‡?(083) 2?; -5*'; (?*.;]‡ 5(9) 2?; -5*'; 4?3.
  ]6;46* ‡(28*85;4, 0‡);;(85)?(8):‡?)887

- Every episode of *Gravity Falls* (a middle school-friendly animated video series) includes a cryptogram that can be solved with one of more of the following ciphers: Ceasar, Atbash, A1Z26, and Vignere's. Here is one example from the first episode:

  Zhofrph wr Judylwb Idoov

- For a very exciting codes lesson full of action, try learning to communicate with semaphore (flag signals). Caution: This code involves an incredible amount of movement and is best practiced in the gym or outdoors on opposite sides of a field.
- The Lego Bionicle universe contains a few interesting codes that get students' brains thinking in symbols rather than letters. Try solving this message in Matoran:

Figure 15.2 Matoran Code Example

LESSON 15

Lesson 16

Breaking Out

Objective

Students will demonstrate cooperative problem-solving skills and recognize each other's strengths.

Rationale

This magical lesson involves some careful planning but pays off big time in excitement and collaboration. Your goal is to facilitate an experience similar to an escape room where various clues and puzzles all work together to allow a team to "break out", solve a mystery, and receive a reward. It incorporates movement as students actively search for clues around the room and open locks. Mingling happens when students spontaneously

DOI: 10.4324/9781003657163-20

collaborate and share ideas. The made-to-order aspect of this lesson is what makes it so useful again and again no matter what content you are learning.

There are many companies that sell premade breakout games, kits, and mysteries for adults and children that you can purchase and potentially adapt. However, the most meaningful breakout activities I have ever done with middle school students were all custom-made with a few programmable locks and classroom materials. They were based on my current curriculum, and tailored to my students' unique strengths. You can use a breakout lesson to review or preview any academic content, but it is also incredibly powerful for teaching teamwork and collaborative problem-solving. One of the hardest parts of facilitating this lesson is carefully observing your students' struggle without directly helping them. If you manage to do this and have created a sufficiently engaging mystery, they begin to seek out and rely on each other instead of you. The social value of this productive struggle is priceless!

Standards

NAGC 3.5. Instructional Strategies. Students with gifts and talents become independent investigators.

NAGC 4.2. Social Competence. Students with gifts and talents develop social competence manifested in positive peer relationships and social interactions.

Preparation

Lesson Duration: 20–60 minutes

Materials Required: locks, lockable boxes, printed clues, timer, reward, rubric

Background and Setup 30–60 minutes: Create three to four puzzles with clues from the content you wish to preview or review. Design the breakout with your students' cultures and strengths in mind. Each clue should lead to a solution that opens a lock. Lock your reward sign and/or prize into a box and add a hasp to use multiple locks. Hide clues around the room. Print copies of the rubric if you plan to assess student problem-solving or collaboration skills.

Step-by-step Facilitation

1. Issue a challenge to the class by clearly stating the objective of the breakout, how many items are hidden, and how many times you will offer a hint if they get stuck. If there are any unfamiliar locks, make sure students know how to operate them. If you will be scoring on a rubric, make sure students have seen it before.
2. Set a timer and allow students to work together to "break out". Letting them struggle is the most challenging but important part.
3. Observe who is trying what strategy and take notes. Use a problem-solving rubric for individuals or the whole class.
4. Offer hints only when the whole group agrees they are stuck. Collect opened locks once they are removed.
5. When students Break Out and get the box opened, pause the timer, congratulate them, and sit everyone down for the debrief. See the upcoming Assessment and Closure section for specific guidance on conducting a productive debrief.
6. If students do not Break Out, conduct the alternate debrief.

Tips for a Successful Lesson

- **Nonlinear Clues Work Best**

  Create a number of clues that is appropriate for the number of students who are solving the game together. Include at least one clue for every two students, ensuring there are enough different puzzles to work on for everyone. Try to avoid the typical linear scavenger hunt-style clues where one must be solved to get to another. When multiple groups of students are solving different clues at once, they are more likely to stay engaged and the debrief can be more constructive at the end of the game.

- **Keep Them Moving**

  The physical aspects of this activity are critical. Hide the clues in several surprising places all over the room in locations high and low (put the clues in brightly colored or labeled envelopes that match so they will know when they have found something important). This allows some students to stop and solve while others keep searching. Another important aspect of movement is that finding clues and solutions should allow them to physically manipulate objects like locks, cipher wheels, UV lights, and puzzle pieces. Try adding background music or changing the lighting if this will help engage students more in the excitement.

- **Limited Number of Hints**

  Before the timer starts, announce how many hints are available. Sometimes they will get stuck and have no idea how to continue. If everyone in the group agrees to use one of the hints, pause the timer and announce your hint clearly to all. Help them just enough to get the action going again. Then restart the timer, and get back to quietly observing again.

- **A Meaningful Reward**

  Whatever you decide to hide in the largest box to end the game is important because not everyone in your group will be motivated in the same way. Often gifted learners are curious enough to want to solve a good mystery for its own sake or even just to see the locks come open. Unfortunately, in my experience, not everyone is equally motivated by a "We Broke Out" sign and photo op. For this reason, I choose the rewards to match the needs of my most demanding detectives. This means sometimes I hide snacks or stickers in the box and sometimes there are passes for extra credit or an outdoor workday. The most difficult challenge of all comes when students don't break out. If they don't break out, they don't get the reward. This is a tough but fair lesson appropriate for middle school. In this case, the debrief must be handled especially carefully with explanations and encouragement. If it is your first time ever trying a breakout activity, make it sufficiently challenging, but keep in mind they will need a small victory to motivate them to try a more difficult mystery next time.

- **Debrief and Reset**

  Please don't ever skip the debrief discussion no matter how much they want to celebrate and relax after solving a super challenging mystery. Students need to hear their specific individual accomplishments reflected back by you and their peers. This will further cement their trust in each other and help them practice giving and receiving compliments. After the debrief, let them help reset the locks and re-hide the clues for the next group. They will love to be part of the action and it will save you time.

Made-to-order Mysteries

Interdisciplinary units are perfect for breakout activities because the clues and solutions can come from a wide variety of subjects and involve mathematical and language-based thinking. However, even a very standardized review of a specific topic can be turned into a fun and exciting breakout game when you add custom ciphers, invisible ink, an image cut apart like a jigsaw puzzle, or math problems with your students' names. Try writing clues that specifically appeal to the culture, talents, or interests of individual learners. Do you have someone in your class who loves sports stats, speaks Spanish, knows how to read music, or memorizes K-pop lyrics? Incorporate clues that showcase that strength and watch their eyes light up! Generative AI tools can help you write clues quickly connecting a variety of content with student interests, but be careful to test everything out first and evaluate it all for potential bias and accuracy. Have fun creating and solving an active classroom mystery.

Assessment and Closure

During the "We Broke Out" debrief, each student must recognize another student who successfully found a hidden clue, solved a puzzle, opened a lock, or collaborated with someone else. Give time to think before responding if this is new for them. Provide sentence starters for recognizing each other's strengths and complimenting hard work and success. Use your notes or the rubric to guide the discussion if needed. Continue sharing until all students have been recognized. Students can reset locks and re-hide clues for another group if time remains.

During the alternative "We Almost Broke Out" debrief, each student should recognize one success from another person AND take ownership for a personal way they could have improved their collaboration or problem-solving techniques. Helping students understand failure as a learning opportunity is critical. What will they do differently next time?

Differentiation Ideas

Add more locks, clues, and/or red herrings to make the breakout more complex. Remove locks, add extra clues, or remove red herrings to make the breakout simpler. Adjust the expectations on your problem-solving or collaboration rubric as needed.

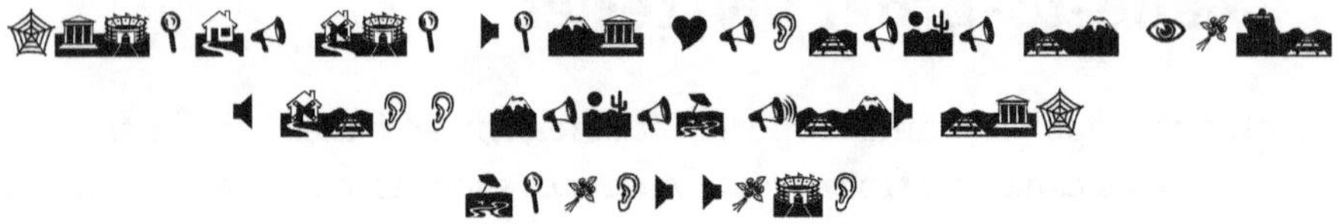

Resource 16.1 Ready for Monday Lesson – Simple Medieval Europe Breakout

Materials Required

printed clues, envelopes, padlock with key, three-digit number lock, four-digit number lock, five-letter word lock, directional lock, hasp, large box, and prizes (optional)

Clues and Solutions

Lock Used	Clue(s) Used	Solution Explanation	Correct Lock Combination
Word Lock	Rebus Puzzle Riddle	I hold both charms and iron gate, where Medieval men dine and servants wait. Speak my name and I may convey, the children's politest way. Two meanings walk through just one door. What am I?	Manor
Padlock and Key	Magna Carta	Read the Magna Carta summary and look for missing letters.	The key can be found in the leaves
Four-Digit Lock	Important Figures and Dates	Solve the math problem using the dates given in the chart. 750/13 = 57.7 57.7 × 19 = 1,096	1,096
Directional Lock	Events/Discoveries Outside Europe	Follow the events in chronological order across the map. East, South, East, West, East	Right, Down, Right, Left, Right
Three-Digit Lock	AI Bubonic Plague Summary	Decode crossword clues using A1Z26 cipher. Complete the puzzle and encode the answers using the same cipher.	E I A 591

Setup

1. Print and cut apart all necessary clues.
2. Place each clue into a separate envelope and hide them in five different locations around the classroom.

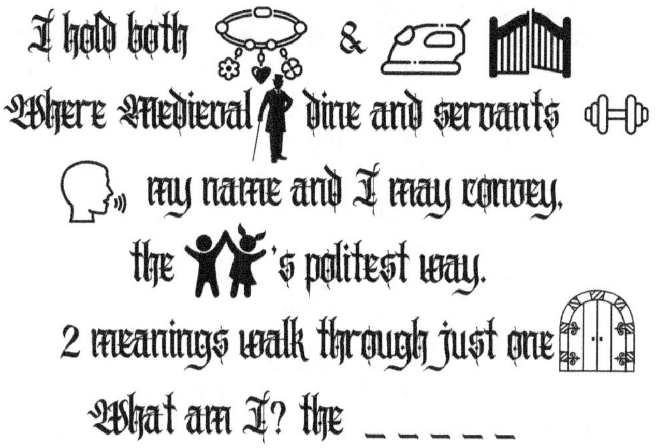

Figure 16.1 Medieval Breakout Rebus Clue

3. Set each lock to the correct code listed previously. Hide the padlock key in the leaves of a plant, tree, or under a picture of something with leaves.
4. Place prizes and a "We Broke Out" sign into the large box. Place the hasp on the box and secure with all five locks. Place the box in a visible location.

Summary of the Magna Carta as sealed by King John on June 15, 1215 at Runnymede, England

I is accordingly our wis and command that the nglish Church shall be free, and that men in our ingdom shall hav and keep all these liberties, rights, and concessions, well and peaceabl in their fullness and entirety for them and their heirs, of us and our heirs, in all things and all places for ever.

No man shall be for ed to perform more service for knight's 'fee', or other free holding of la d, than is due from it.

To any man whom we have deprived or dispossessed of lands, castles, li rties, or rights, without the law ul judgement f his eq als, we will at o ce restore these.

For a trivial offence, a free man shall be fine only proportion to he degree of is off nce, and for a serious offence corresponding y, but not so h avily s to depri him of hi livelihood.

Most common people in the Medieval times lived an average of 30–35 years. Find the average age of these important figures then multiply it by the age of the youngest to die as a martyr.

Name	Lifespan	Significance
Charlemagne	747–814	King of the Franks; crowned Holy Roman Emperor in 800, united much of Western Europe
William the Conqueror	1028–1087	Duke of Normandy; led the Norman conquest of England in 1066
Eleanor of Aquitaine	1122–1204	Queen of France and England; powerful political figure and patron of the arts
Thomas Aquinas	1225–1274	Dominican friar and theologian; major figure in scholasticism
Joan of Arc	1412–1431	French heroine/martyr during the Hundred Years' War
Geoffrey Chaucer	c. 1343–1400	English poet; author of *The Canterbury Tales*
Richard the Lionheart	1157–1199	King of England; famed military leader during the Crusades
Saladin	c. 1137–1193	Muslim leader who recaptured Jerusalem during the Crusades
Pope Urban II	c. 1035–1099	Launched the First Crusade in 1095
Hildegard of Bingen	1098–1179	Abbess, composer, and mystic; one of the most influential women of the Middle Ages
Thomas Becket	c. 1119–1170	Archbishop of Canterbury; murdered after conflict with King Henry II
Isabella I of Castile	1451–1504	United Spain and sponsored Columbus's voyage
Marco Polo	1254–1324	Venetian traveler who journeyed to Asia

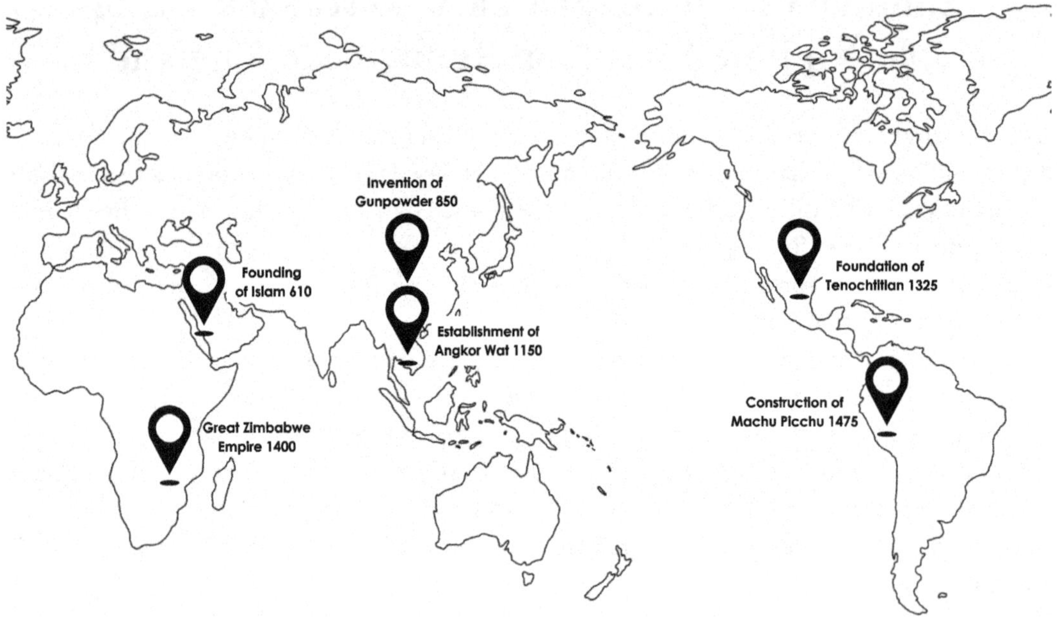

Figure 16.2 Medieval Breakout Map Clue

Figure 16.3 Medieval Breakout Crossword Clue

1-3-18-15-19-19

2. 14-9-3-11-14-1-13-5 6–15-18 20-8-5 16-12-1-7-21-5

7. 20-18-1-4-5 18-15-21-20-5 20-8-1-20 8–5-12-16-5-4 19-16-18-5-1-4 20-8-5 4–9-19-5-1-19-5

10. 16-18-1-3-20-9-3-5 15-6 9–19-15-12-1-20-9-14-7 20-8-5 19-9-3-11

11. 16-12-1-7-21-5 13-1-19-11-19 23-15-18-14 2–25 4–15-3-20-15-18-19 23-5-18-5 6–9-12-12-5-4 23-9-20-8 8–5-18-2-19 1–14-4 18-5-19-5-13-2-12-5-4 20-8-9-19

12. 18-5-12-9-7-9-15-21-19 7–18-15-21-16 15-6-20-5-14 16-5-18-19-5-3-21-20-5-4 1–14-4 19-3-1-16-5-7-15-1-20-5-4 4–21-18-9-14-7 20-8-5 16-12-1-7-21-5

4-15-23-14

1. 2–1-3-20-5-18-9-1 20-8-1-20 3–1-21-19-5-4 20-8-5 2–21-2-15-14-9-3 16-12-1-7-21-5

3. 3–9-20-25 9–14 5–14-7-12-1-14-4 20-8-1-20 12-15-19-20 1 12-1-18-7-5 16-15-18-20-9-15-14 15-6 9–20-19 16-15-16-21-12-1-20-9-15-14

LESSON 16

4. 19-15-3-9-1-12 7–18-15-21-16 8–9-20 8–1-18-4-5-19-20 2–25 20-8-5 16-12-1-7-21-5 4–21-5 20-15 16-15-15-18 12-9-22-9-14-7 3–15-14-4-9-20-9-15-14-19
5. 9–14-19-5-3-20 20-8-1-20 20-18-1-14-19-13-9-20-20-5-4 20-8-5 16-12-1-7-21-5 20-15 8–21-13-1-14-19
6. 3–15-21-14-20-18-25 20-8-1-20 12-15-19-20 8–1-12-6 9–20-19 16-15-16-21-12-1-20-9-15-14
8. 16-1-9-14-6-21-12 19-23-15-12-12-5-14 12-25-13-16-8 14-15-4-5-19 20-8-1-20 23-5-18-5 1 3–12-1-19-19-9-3 16-12-1-7-21-5 19-25-13-16-20-15-13
9. 1–14-9-13-1-12 15-6-20-5-14 2–12-1-13-5-4 6–15-18 19-16-18-5-1-4-9-14-7 20-8-5 16-12-1-7-21-5

Lesson 17

Sequencing A Timeline

Objective

Students will make predictions then correctly organize a series of events to create a timeline or story.

Rationale

This lesson gives students a chance to analyze a series of events and place them into an evolving order on a timeline considering both causes and effects. It also asks them to make predictions and correct initial assumptions. All this deep thinking happens while students are actively discussing the concepts with each other and moving around the room to create a large physical project that can be cleared away in under a minute or remain part of your classroom décor indefinitely.

 DOI: 10.4324/9781003657163-21

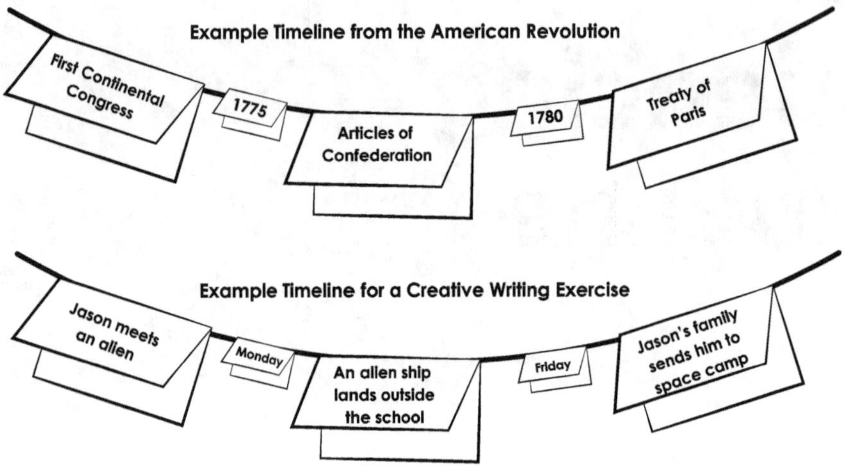

Figure 17.1 Example Timelines

Recent studies in cognitive psychology have demonstrated that making a prediction prior to fully understanding a concept is a powerful learning tool (Brod, 2021; Carvalho et al., 2018). Our brains want to know if our predictions are accurate and are especially attentive to remember surprising or corrected information. This lesson capitalizes on the middle school magic of socialized predicting and correcting in an active hands-on exercise. It is especially useful when studying history, but can be customized to almost any content area.

Standards

NAGC 1.5. Cognitive, Psychosocial, and Affective Growth. Students with gifts and talents demonstrate cognitive growth and psychosocial skills that support their talent development as a result of meaningful and challenging learning activities that address their unique characteristics and needs.

NAGC 3.5. Instructional Strategies. Students with gifts and talents become independent investigators.

NAGC 4.2. Social Competence. Students with gifts and talents develop social competence manifested in positive peer relationships and social interactions.

Preparation

Lesson Duration: 30–50 minutes

Materials Required: String, Set of Folded Papers with Events or Images, and Set of Folded Cardstock Date Markers

Background and Setup 20–30 minutes: Prepare a set of folded papers with events or images labeled identically on two sides. Prepare a set of smaller date markers on folded cards (optional: prepare a set of hints that will help students correctly sequence the events). Attach the string to opposite walls of your classroom so it stretches as far as possible across the room just above the heads of the students.

Step-by-step Facilitation

1. Divide the class into partners.
2. Distribute Event Papers and Date Markers evenly so each pair of students has a random assortment of Events and Dates.
3. Ask each pair of students to predict the order of the few Events and Dates they have in front of them by sequencing them on the desktop. Move around the room as students are sequencing their cards to answer questions and get a sense of their current understanding.
4. Explain that the string over their heads will become a giant timeline eventually including every Event and Date.
5. Ask each pair to make a prediction about where one of their Events or Dates will go on the larger timeline. One student at a time should get up and place one paper or card over the string at the predicted location explaining why they think it belongs there.
6. At this point do not correct students, just listen carefully to their thinking.
7. Combine partners into groups of four students. Each pair should bring their remaining events and date markers to the new group and combine them. Leave the predicted Events and Dates as placed on the timeline.
8. If using clues, reveal one clue at this point. Groups now discuss and re-sequence their newly combined set of events and dates on a desktop.

9. After the new sequences are ordered, ask if anyone wants to change the position of an earlier prediction. Allow anyone who previously placed a marker on the large timeline to move it.
10. Then ask each group to make a prediction about where two of their Events or Dates will go on the larger timeline. Two students should get up and place these papers in their predicted place while explaining their reasoning. They may slide other events and date cards around if needed.
11. Combine groups again and repeat the process of hint, sequence, correct, and predict until the entire timeline is completed and everyone in the class has had a chance to place and move items on the timeline.
12. Reveal any final corrections if accurate sequencing is necessary. Then debrief with the class. What made predicting a correct placement difficult? What does it mean when there are gaps in the timeline or when many cards are clustered together? Did any event papers belong correctly in more than one place? How were the date markers helpful or not? How does it feel to only know part of the story? How would this activity be different if you had to sequence all the dates and events on your own without talking to anyone?

Tips for a Successful Lesson

- **Plenty of Space**

  This lesson works really well in a large space with room to move around freely between the furniture. If your classroom is small or a bit cramped, consider borrowing a larger classroom or using a common area. This activity also works well outdoors between two trees when there is not too much wind. If changing locations is not an option, ask students to move their desks toward the outer walls to allow as much movement around the timeline as possible without tripping.

- **Making Predictions Means Making Mistakes**

  The magic of this lesson is built on making a prediction without having all the information and doing so in a fairly public way. As explained previously, this will prepare students' brains to remember the correct information longer. This cycle of predicting and correcting is a perfect time to reinforce the idea that making mistakes is often the most important part of learning. To help reduce my students' anxiety and perfectionism, I assure them that I will not be grading their timeline placement until we are all satisfied at the end of the lesson. I also model how to gracefully correct a mistake by intentionally placing an event incorrectly at the end of round one and talking about my thinking as I adjust it in round two. Then when I offer a chance for anyone else to make a public correction it feels more natural and sometimes we even applaud each other for making mistakes that help everyone learn.

Assessment and Closure

End this lesson with a narrative or expository writing exercise focusing on cause and effect. It should include at least three events from the class timeline and provide an analytical summary in one page or less. Keep the timeline hanging and allow students to move around the room to view it as they work on their writing. Score the final writing exercise on a rubric.

Differentiation Ideas

As mentioned previously, this lesson can be easily adapted from a history lesson into the realm of language arts instead. It can be a review lesson after reading a novel or an idea generation session for creative writing by using events that could occur in a complex story. In this last case, there will be more than one accurate way to order the events! This flexibility makes for dozens of different timeline possibilities, so you should be prepared for a rich discussion of plot development techniques and a potentially heated debate over when certain events should occur.

To extend this lesson for your most advanced learners, consider including discrepant events from other disciplines or parts of the world. For example, in a timeline of the American Revolution, include scientific discoveries or significant events from African and Asian countries that also occurred near the end of the 18th century.

To support students who may not be as familiar with the timeline events, you can ask them to select key events from the list to research and create more detailed event papers prior to class including dates and significance of each. You can also provide more details on each event paper yourself or provide more details in your list of clues.

Example Events for a Timeline of the American Revolution

Label event papers without the dates for students. Keep this list as the answer key. Create date cards labeled 1760, 1765, 1770, 1775, 1780, 1785.

Proclamation of 1763 – British ban on colonial settlement west of the Appalachian Mountains.

Sugar Act (1764) – First British law taxing the colonies to raise revenue.

Stamp Act (1765) – Tax on printed materials; sparked widespread protests.

Stamp Act Congress (1765) – First unified colonial response to British taxation.

Declaratory Act (1766) – Asserted Britain's right to legislate for the colonies "in all cases".

Townshend Acts (1767) – Imposed duties on imported goods; reignited boycotts.

Boston Massacre (1770) – British soldiers killed five colonists during a confrontation.

Tea Act (1773) – Allowed the British East India Company to sell tea directly to colonies, undercutting local merchants.

Boston Tea Party (1773) – Colonists dumped British tea into Boston Harbor in protest.

Intolerable Acts (1774) – Harsh laws passed by Britain to punish Massachusetts.

First Continental Congress (1774) – Colonial leaders met to coordinate resistance to British policy.

Battles of Lexington and Concord (April 1775) – First military engagements of the Revolution.

Second Continental Congress (May 1775) – Took charge of the war effort and created the Continental Army.

Battle of Bunker Hill (June 1775) – Early battle showing colonial resolve despite British victory.

Olive Branch Petition (July 1775) – Final attempt at peace rejected by King George III.

Common Sense Published (January 1776) – Thomas Paine's pamphlet encouraged independence.

Declaration of Independence (July 4, 1776) – Formal statement of colonial separation from Britain.

Battle of Long Island (August 1776) – Major British victory; Washington's forces narrowly escaped.

Battle of Trenton (December 1776) – Washington's surprise attack revived American morale.

Battle of Saratoga (October 1777) – Turning point; led to French alliance.

Valley Forge Winter (1777–1778) – Harsh winter of training and perseverance for the Continental Army.

France Enters the War (February 1778) – France allies with the U.S. after Saratoga.

Benedict Arnold's Treason (1780) – American general's failed plot to surrender West Point.

Battle of Camden (August 1780) – British victory in the Southern campaign.

Battle of Cowpens (January 1781) – Key American victory in the South.

Battle of Guilford Courthouse (March 1781) – British won but suffered heavy losses.

Siege of Yorktown (October 1781) – Final major battle; British General Cornwallis surrendered.

Articles of Confederation Ratified (1781) – First constitution of the United States.

Treaty of Paris Signed (1783) – Officially ended the war; recognized U.S. independence.

Discrepant Events for Additional Challenge:

Founding of the Qing Dynasty's Canton System (1760) – The Chinese government limited foreign trade to the port of Canton, restricting Western access to Chinese goods.

James Cook begins Second Voyage to Antarctica (1772) – Captain Cook crossed the Antarctic circle and mapped much of the South Pacific.

Pugachev's Rebellion (1773) – A massive peasant uprising against Catherine the Great in Russia.

First Xhosa War Begins (1779) – Kingdom of Xhosa in modern-day South Africa battled European settlers, beginning the longest running military resistance against colonialism in Africa.

Túpac Amaru II's Rebellion (1780) – A major indigenous uprising led by Túpac Amaru II against Spanish colonial rule and oppression that erupted in modern-day Peru.

Example Events for a Creative Writing Timeline

Label event papers for students. There is no correct order for the events of this story and students may debate. Create date cards labeled with each day of the week.

Jason accidentally microwaves his retainer and opens a portal in the school cafeteria.

A substitute teacher communicates only in binary code when supervising detention.

Jason's reflection starts winking at him, independently.

An alien ship lands on the football field during lunch, and nobody else seems to notice.

Jason discovers that the school mascot costume is not empty – ever.

The vending machine gives Jason a glowing cookie labeled "DO NOT EAT".

Jason meets an alien named "Xorvlak" hiding in a locker in the boys' locker room.

Xorvlak offers to help Jason with his algebra homework using telepathy.

Jason's cat starts speaking Spanish and warning him about "the glowing ones".

Jason's friends think he's going crazy.

A glowing trail of slime leads Jason to the janitor's closet, which contains a secret elevator.

Xorvlak's spaceship needs fuel.

Jason's backpack starts floating, humming the *Star Wars* theme.

The alien ship lands again outside the school – this time with Xorvlak's angry parents on board.

Jason's family signs him up for space camp.

Jason uncovers a buried capsule labeled "RETURN TO ALPHA SECTOR 7".

Jason wakes up with a barcode tattoo on his elbow that wasn't there the night before.

The bio lab's pet turtle glows under moonlight and seems to whisper ancient prophecies.

An old yearbook in the library from 1972 shows Jason's photo – despite him not being born yet.

Jason tries to warn his classmates, but they all start speaking in binary.

The Wi-Fi cuts out and strange symbols start appearing on every screen.

The drama club's production of *Grease* is taken over by real extraterrestrials and it's amazing.

Jason learns he's part alien on his mom's side and must pass an intergalactic driving test.

Xorvlak invites Jason to his home planet for prom.

Jason saves the school from an alien invasion using only a kazoo, a glow stick, and an old copy of George Orwell's *The War of the Worlds*.

Lesson 18

Describe and Build

Objective

Students will utilize speaking and listening skills to construct a replica of a hidden object.

Rationale

This lesson will test even the best communicators in your classroom, but it is also a highly motivating thinking challenge. The magic here is in the teamwork and in learning to rely on others who have more information. Your builders will be so excited for the simple joy of constructing something with hands-on materials. They will be ready to concentrate, pay attention to details, and ask clarifying questions. The describers realize quickly that they have all the answers and just have to find the best way to explain the mystery to the builders who are anxious to get the most accurate description possible.

 DOI: 10.4324/9781003657163-22

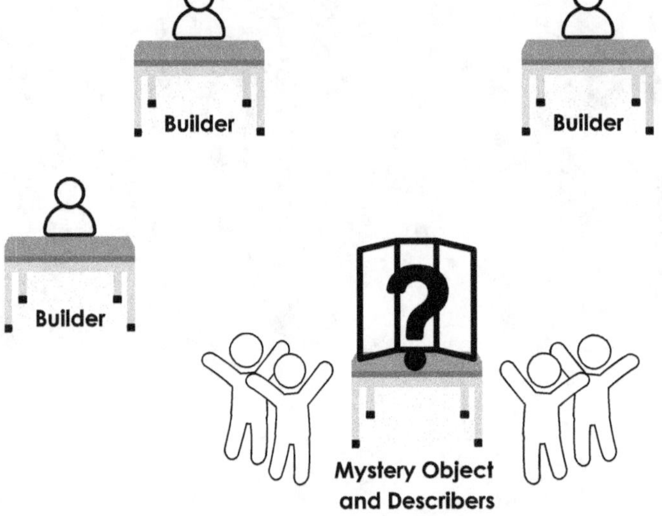

Figure 18.1 Describe and Build Classroom Setup

As you watch the describers rush back and forth to check and double check the mystery object, you'll see how incorporating movement and mystery helps them concentrate so much harder on the simple task of communication. The builders have a very limited amount of information but all the responsibility to actually create a successful replication of the mystery object. Their power lies in listening and asking clarifying questions.

My favorite part of this activity is the excitement on each person's face when the first mystery object is finally revealed and they realize how close they were to the original design. Then almost everyone is very motivated to switch roles and prove that they can be a more effective describer or builder than their partner as you start construction of mystery object two. Capitalize on this magical moment by asking both the builders and describers to name something their partner did that was really helpful (gestures, questioning, explaining the big picture first, etc.). Try to avoid unhelpful criticism while nudging them toward this natural discovery of the most effective communication skills.

Standards

NAGC 4.2. Social Competence. Students with gifts and talents develop social competence manifested in positive peer relationships and social interactions.

NAGC 4.5. Communication Competence. Students with gifts and talents develop competence in interpersonal and technical communication skills. They demonstrate advanced oral and written skills and creative expression.

Preparation

Lesson Duration: 20–30 minutes

Materials Required: Construction materials appropriate for the challenge level desired (Lego, KNEX, etc.).

Background and Setup 30–45 minutes: Organize construction materials into complete sets of identical pieces with one set per team plus two extra sets. Construct and hide two different mystery objects using the extra sets of materials. Time yourself making the mystery objects and double that number for student timing. Keep the number of construction pieces to around 10–15 maximum. If utilizing a rubric, make sure students have access to view it prior to the activity.

Step-by-step Facilitation

1. Divide class into partners.
2. Each pair should determine who will be the first describer and who will be the first builder. They will switch these roles later. Distribute a set of construction materials to each builder.
3. Allow time for the describers to view the mystery object at the front of the room, behind a barrier, while the builders familiarize themselves with the construction materials at their seat.
4. Start the timer and send the describers back to their team.
5. Builders begin and complete the construction according to specifications given by the describers. Describers may only coach the builder. They may not touch any construction materials. Builders may not view the mystery object.
6. Allow describers to come back and check the mystery object as often as needed.
7. When time is up, reveal the mystery object and allow teams to check their work

8. Debrief with the group. What terms or guidance was most helpful from the describers? What did the builders wish they would have known?
9. Switch roles and repeat this process with mystery object 2.
10. Debrief and note improvements in communication when both partners have already experienced the other role (shared experience builds trust).

Tips for a Successful Lesson

- **Spread Out**

  Try to make sure your builders are located as far apart as possible around the room and definitely not sharing a workstation with another builder. This will help everyone keep their eyes on their own build. Checking to see what others are doing is natural, but blatant copying should be discouraged.

- **Keep It Organized**

  Keep each identical set of materials organized into bags or tubs. Make sure you allow time for deconstruction and cleanup at the end of class, so the materials are all returned and ready to use again in another class.

- **Incorporate Music**

  Use your classroom playlist or select a set of songs without words that can cover the chatter of the different groups. Turning on and off the music can also signal the difference between build time and teacher instructions or the end of the activity.

- **Level Up With Creativity**

  Once your students are familiar with the rules of this activity, you can dramatically increase the level of challenge by inviting the describers to create their own mystery object as long as you have plenty of materials. This also works well if you have multiple partitions, a back room, or even hallway space to hide them while they are creating. They should be required to use every piece and try to be as unique as possible.

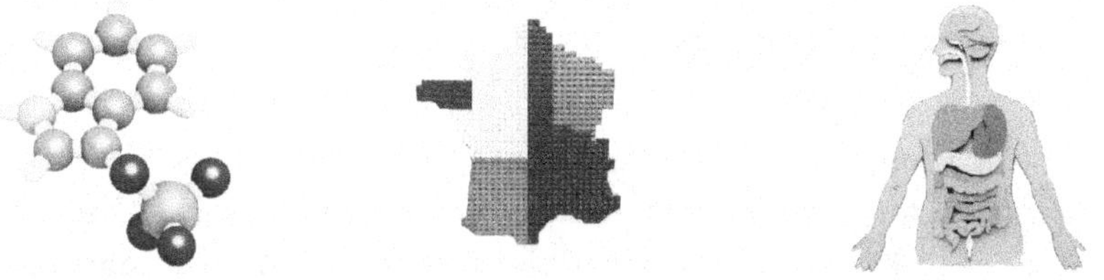

3D Molecule **Lego Country Map** **Cardstock Body System**

Figure 18.2 Mystery Object Examples

Made-to-order Mystery

When customizing this lesson to your subject area and current content, first consider the building materials you have available in appropriate quantities. Legos are a wonderfully versatile construction tool, but there is no need to limit yourself to constructing only with one fairly expensive type of material. Pipe cleaners and pony beads can become molecular models. Tape and construction paper can become a digestive system, a political map, flag, or a three-dimensional graph. If you have the budget to purchase materials, Keva blocks, KNex, and Wikki Stix also make excellent construction tools.

Next think carefully about the aspects of your curriculum that can be best understood as a system of interconnected parts where the quantity, color, location, or connections between individual parts has an important meaning. If it is a concept that could be tested on a labeling worksheet, this activity will be so much more powerful and more fun! Practice constructing each mystery object yourself with a timer, then double that to estimate how long it should reasonably take your students. Let your own creativity take the lead and give yourself permission to play while constructing two different mystery objects that are meaningful and fun to build.

Assessment and Closure

Allow students to self-assess their speaking and listening skills after the activity. See **Resource 18.1 Mystery Object Communication and Construction Rubric** for an example.

Differentiation Ideas

To increase the challenge, allow the describers to view the object only once at the beginning. Increasing the number of construction pieces also increases the complexity. To provide support prior to or during the activity, provide a visual key naming each piece and examples of how to describe the ways they can be connected.

Mystery Object Communication and Construction Rubric

Criteria	3 - Exceeds Expectations	2 - Meets Expectations	1 - Below Expectations
Listening Skills	Listens attentively to all verbal directions and asks clarifying questions when needed. Demonstrates excellent understanding of the instructions.	Listens to most verbal directions and occasionally asks clarifying questions. Demonstrates satisfactory understanding of the instructions.	Frequently interrupts or does not listen to verbal directions. Demonstrates limited understanding of the instructions.
Verbal Communication	Speaks clearly and concisely when providing feedback or asking questions. Uses appropriate vocabulary and tone.	Speaks clearly most of the time and uses appropriate vocabulary, but may occasionally stumble or use an inappropriate tone.	Speaks unclearly, uses inappropriate vocabulary, or has difficulty communicating effectively.
Mystery Object Construction	Constructs the mystery object accurately and precisely, following the verbal directions. The final product matches the description provided.	Constructs the mystery object with minor inaccuracies or deviations from the verbal directions. The final product is mostly consistent with the description provided.	Constructs the mystery object with significant inaccuracies or deviations from the verbal directions. The final product does not match the description provided.

Lesson 19

Rubik's Cube Mosaic

Objective

Students will create and solve visual puzzles using 3 × 3 Rubik's cubes.

Rationale

This exciting activity combines art and play into a highly engaging cooperative problem-solving challenge. Cubes can be expensive to purchase in large quantities, but this lesson works well even with just nine puzzle cubes. Students will work together to create a mystery mosaic image that can only be revealed when all the correct cube configurations are placed together.

Try to choose images that are colorful but simple and connect to a recognizable concept within the curriculum. If introducing a new idea,

 DOI: 10.4324/9781003657163-23

or if it is the first time groups have attempted this challenge, the mosaic design will need to be relatively simple, such as the flag for a particular country or a mathematical symbol such as pi. If we are reviewing images that students should know, I can make the pattern more challenging and detailed, and this also makes for a more exciting mystery. Examples of a more complex image would be a double-helix DNA strand or a simple system of equations.

Your middle school gifted students will enjoy the physical aspect of manipulating the cubes while also considering their own cube's place within the larger puzzle. This activity is especially wonderful for highlighting the skills of visual-spatial thinkers who will naturally become the leaders, helping to solve the larger puzzle. This challenge also requires strong communication skills as students mingle and move their unique parts of the design into place.

Taking photos of the completed mosaic and/or creating a time lapse video of the mosaic coming together will add even more excitement and importance to the artistic creation. Even students who don't like to be photographed tend to appreciate watching their hands-on camera solving one side of a cube and connecting it correctly with the others. Studying the photo or time lapse can allow a productive debriefing discussion where the group can point out times of struggle and breakthroughs. When watching the time lapse, I encourage students to compliment each other by pausing and asking something like, "Who just figured out that red section? How did you know it should be turned that way?" This allows them freedom to verbalize their thinking, ultimately recognizing patterns that lead to solutions.

Standards

NAGC 3.5. Instructional Strategies. Students with gifts and talents become independent investigators.

NAGC 4.5 Communication Competence. Educators ensure access to advanced communication tools, including assistive technologies, and use of these tools for expressing higher-level thinking and creative productivity.

Preparation

Lesson Duration: 20–60 minutes

Materials Required: Nine-plus Rubik's cubes, one or more per student, Printed Mosaics, (Optional: camera with time lapse and tripod)

Background and Setup 30–60 minutes: Make sure you and your students know how to solve at least one side of a Rubik's cube prior to this activity. Use the free printable materials available at Rubiks.com or any of the numerous video tutorials available online. It is not necessary for them to know how to solve the whole cube.

Print and cut apart a mosaic that is sized to the number of cubes you plan to use. Mosaic designs should be relevant to curriculum content or individual creative expression of student interests.

Use the mosaic generator at Ruwix.com (https://ruwix.com/rubiks-cube-mosaic-generator/) if needed. Alternatively, have students design their own secret mosaics using Pixilart (https://www.pixilart.com/) or Google Sheets. Remember that if you are using standard cubes, the art can only be depicted using the six traditional cube colors of white, yellow, red, orange, blue, and green. Print the mosaic patterns and cut them apart into sections that are 3 × 3 squares so each pattern piece represents one cube.

If using the team problem-solving rubric, provide a copy to students.

Step-by-step Facilitation

1. Distribute cubes and pattern pieces to individuals or partners at desks.
2. Students will need to manipulate their cubes until they are correctly solved on one side to match the provided pattern, then each can be brought to the larger puzzle.
3. Allow students to work together around a larger central table to solve the larger mystery puzzle image. Optional: Set up a tripod and camera with time lapse to capture the action at this table over time.
4. Provide guidance as needed to individuals or ask for volunteer cubing coaches who can advise their peers without touching.
5. If you have enough cubes, allow students to solve more than one. Everyone should contribute at least one cube to the solution.
6. After the puzzle is solved, debrief to discuss challenges and how they were overcome by the team. Watch the time lapse video if you captured one.

Tips for a Successful Lesson

- **Expect a variety of skill levels**

  Plan ahead for the number of students who will be expert cube solvers and those who may need support. Students who are still learning to solve a side will have more success creating a solid color to add to the larger mosaic, while advanced cubers need the challenge of a complex multicolor pattern. Assign the colored mosaic pattern sections appropriately.

- **Support the Group**

  To provide support for the entire group, mark out an area for the completed mystery mosaic using masking tape. Set out the correct number of cubes to measure appropriate dimensions before distributing them to the class. If teams are struggling to solve the larger image, you can provide a sequence of hints or consider numbering the back of each pattern piece so the numbered pieces create a complete mosaic when arranged numerically left to right, top to bottom.

- **Plan Ahead for Part Two**

  The only time I have regretted using this activity is when I did not anticipate how much students would enjoy it and how eagerly they would demand to try another one! To avoid disappointing your fastest group who are the most effective collaborators, always have a second more difficult set of pattern images ready to go.

- **Incorporate Student Creativity**

  After a few opportunities to try this lesson, your students may be ready to create their own puzzle images. This added layer of creative challenge increases the complexity and motivation! Of course, they want to create a mosaic that is both interesting and difficult for their classmates. Allow one class period for design using graph paper and colored pencils. Multiple drafts will likely be necessary. Before the next class period, copy the completed mosaics in color then cut apart the copies, saving the original for the designer to use as a key. Students can take turns leading the activity while their peers attempt to solve their mystery mosaic.

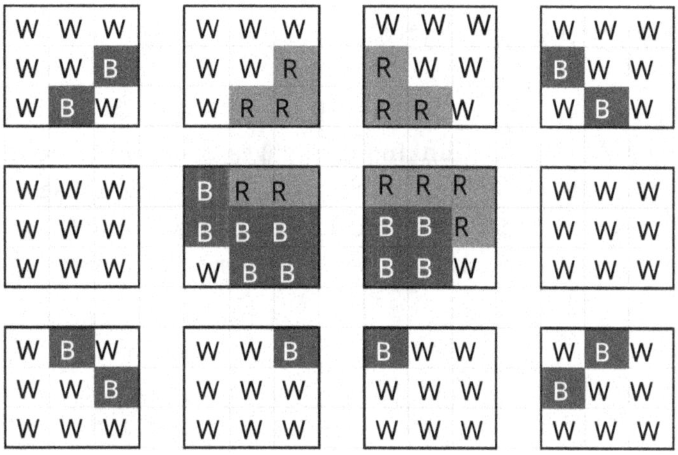

Figure 19.1 Example 12-cube Mosaic Flag of South Korea

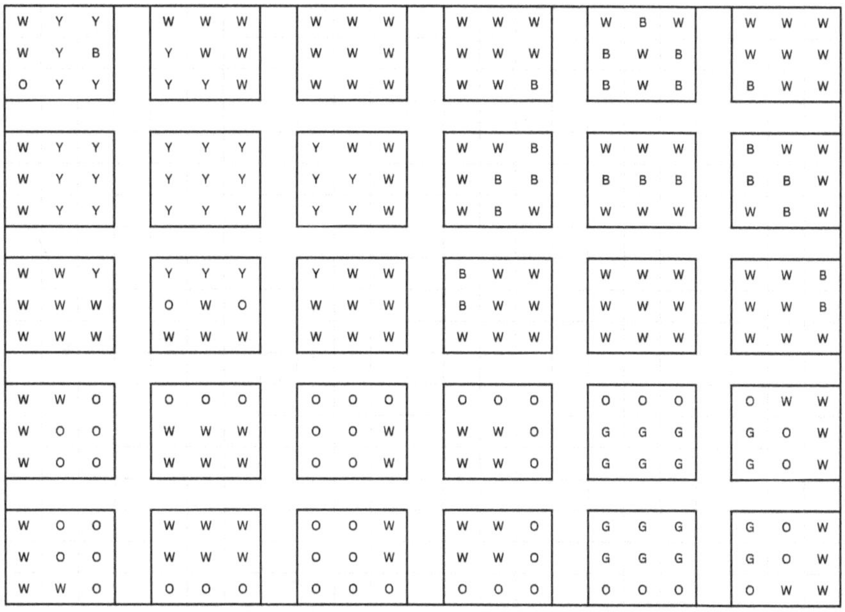

Figure 19.2 Example 30-cube Mosaic Rebus Puzzle Chicago

Assessment and Closure

Watch time-lapse videos to view the teamwork and discuss how each individual contributed to the solution. Assess student groups using a team problem-solving rubric.

Differentiation Ideas

Increasing the number of cubes makes the puzzles more challenging very quickly. Additional thinking challenges can also come in pattern analysis and reflection. To support struggling groups, use a category of mosaic images such as characters, landscapes, animals, or flags. To support individual students, reteach solving one side of a cube with solid colors.

Lesson 20

The Cup Game

Objective

Students will work as a team to correctly answer a series of increasingly challenging questions while strategizing for a decreasing amount of mystery prizes.

Rationale

This lesson is a student favorite for many reasons, but mainly the magical mystery of not knowing what is under all those cups! If you are ready to ask students to do some very difficult thinking and problem-solving but need to get them motivated, the Cup Game is ready to ignite their curiosity and collaborative competitive spirit. You'll be amazed how hard they

 DOI: 10.4324/9781003657163-24

Figure 20.1 The Cup Game Setup

work to get the correct answer and to make sure everyone on their team understands how to explain it.

The Cup Game takes a bit longer to set up than some of the other lessons in this book, but is worth the effort for the mental energy you will see students expend for the entire class period. The psychological phenomena at work here is novelty-seeking or our brains' proclivity for new experiences that bring on dopamine and prime us to learn and remember more (Park et al., 2021). Your students will pay close attention to the questions you ask and to the answers of their peers because you are offering the chance to peek under the cups for both a physical prize and the simple mental joy of discovery.

Standards

NAGC 1.5 Cognitive, Psychosocial, and Affective Growth. Students with gifts and talents demonstrate cognitive growth and psychosocial skills that support their talent development as a result of meaningful and challenging learning activities that address their unique characteristics and needs.

NAGC 3.5. Instructional Strategies. Students with gifts and talents become independent investigators.

NAGC 4.2. Social Competence. Students with gifts and talents develop social competence manifested in positive peer relationships and social interactions.

Preparation

Lesson Duration: 30–45 minutes

Materials Required: Class set of opaque plastic cups, small prizes of varying desirability, set of challenging questions to preview or review current curriculum, small dry-erase boards, markers, and erasers. Spinner, dice, or some other way to randomly select which group will answer.

Background and Setup 20–30 minutes: Gather enough cups and different prizes so there is at least one prize cup available per student. Hide the prizes under the cups before class so the students will notice the overturned cups immediately when they enter the room. Select your challenging questions carefully and prepare them on a slide show if visuals are necessary.

Step-by-step Facilitation

1. Divide the class into teams of three or four students and provide each group with a dry-erase board, markers, and an eraser.
2. Display and review the rules of the game on the board. See **Resource 20.1 Cup Game ACT Math edition** for an example.
3. Pose your first challenging question to the class and allow them to discuss and work on the problem for no more than two minutes.
4. Students should write their team answer on the dry-erase boards and flip them facedown to signal that they are finished.
5. When two minutes have passed or when all teams have flipped their boards, ask all teams to raise their answer boards to show their final response. Then announce the correct answer or display it on the screen. All teams who are correct keep their boards up.
6. Use a spinner or roll a die to select which team (that has answered correctly) gets to explain how they solved the problem or otherwise defend their answer with evidence. Only one person from the team is allowed to share the explanation. (If no teams have answered the question correctly, spend some time explaining it and plan to bring it back later in the lesson.)
7. If they are correct, the person providing the explanation may come to the cup table and select two cups to lift into the air, revealing two prizes. They select their favorite prize to take home, then replace the cups exactly as they were.
8. Repeat steps 3–7 with a new question. This time the person who correctly provides the explanation again gets to select two cups to lift. However, they must try to avoid the empty cup and keep in mind the prize that was previously revealed under another cup.

9. Continue with new questions until everyone in the class has earned a prize or you have reached the end of your question set. No one who has already received a prize is eligible to provide an explanation for their group a second time and receive a second prize.
10. Provide exit tickets for self-reflection.

Tips for a Successful Lesson

- **Stashing Great Mystery Prizes**

  Include as many different small prizes as possible under the cups. The key to creating the mystery is surprising them with variety. There should be some highly desirable prizes. My students like small wrapped candy, a bag of chips, or a squishy stress ball. There should also be at least a few funny and less desirable prizes like a pencil top eraser, a binder clip, or a Band-Aid. You can also include coupons for things like free seating, extra credit, or a prize that is too large to fit inside a cup. When preparing for this activity, I try to clean out random objects from my desk or use the small promotional items I pick up from vendor booths at education conferences.

- **One Correct Answer Please**

  Choose a set of questions that each have a single clearly correct answer. This activity works very well with a high-level math or science practice. If you want a team-building lesson to encourage divergent thinking and multiple answers, check out the chapter in this book called "A Picture Is Worth a Thousand Words". Keep in mind that many high-level STEM problems can be solved correctly in more than one way. If a second group has a different correct explanation, allow another speaker and another prize to be selected.

- **To Swap or To Pass**

  Occasionally, one group will dominate in this lesson either by having the most knowledge or through random chance. If this happens, everyone on that team may end up with a prize before other teams even have one prize. In this case, I suggest allowing the leading team to either swap out one of their prizes by lifting a single cup or to pass their turn to any other team with a correct explanation and a lower number of prizes. This helps end the lesson with almost everyone in the class getting the chance to choose some kind of prize.

Assessment and Closure

Require an exit ticket on a note card or sticky note. What question was especially difficult, but you ultimately figured it out? Who helped you during the cup game and what did they do that you appreciated? In the next class period following the Cup Game provide a more formal curriculum-based assessment covering the content of the questions.

Differentiation Ideas

One way to differentiate this lesson is to intentionally arrange the groups to include a variety of skill levels. This will make it more likely that struggling students have a teammate to get ideas from and one team will be less likely to get all the prizes quickly.

Another way to differentiate for advanced students is by offering a BONUS question to extend each regular question. This is available to all groups every time, but only if they have time remaining after finding an answer to the first question. If their first answer is correct, and their name is drawn, a student can answer the BONUS question to lift three cups instead of two on their turn.

Finally, support can be provided to struggling students by allowing them to use a notes page or other print resources to refer to during the questions. You can also extend the think time to three minutes if it becomes clear that multiple groups are having trouble finishing before the two minutes are up. This time extension combined with the optional bonus question is an easy way to differentiate for learners at both ends of the learning curve.

Appendix
Optional Assessment Tools for Monitoring the Magic

Are you ready to collect some data and give your students feedback? Assessment is an essential component of any gifted education program (Callahan, 2021; Cao et al., 2017). However, it often varies from traditional classroom letter grades and is focused on individual goals and growth related to the abilities and skills for which children are identified. Assigning scores to student performances on the activities in this book is part of the made-to-order magic. Some teachers might decide these experiences are just part of the learning process and should not be formally assessed by putting scores into a gradebook or progress report. Some other teachers may need to document progress on the skills students gain from these lessons. Whether you decide to grade these lessons or not, rubrics can provide meaningful feedback directly to your learners to help them set specific and personal goals for growth (Hattie & Timperley, 2007). This appendix provides several flexible rubrics to assess your students' thinking, collaboration, and communication skills on the types of short-term activities contained in this book. For assessing thinking in longer-term projects, see the excellent tools developed by Hess (2025). Most of the following rubrics are meant to be quickly completed by the students as a self-reflection and one is a tool just for your own use to plan further instruction. Each upcoming instrument can be accessed as a digital version and modified to fit the needs of your classroom.

Team Collaboration and Problem-solving Self-evaluation (Lessons 4, 16, and 19)

Rate your collaboration skills on a five-star scale. Draw the number of stars you think you earned in each box of the criteria column.

My Name ________________________________			
Criteria	**I Rocked It!** *****	**I'm Getting There** ***	**I Need More Practice** *
Team Contribution	I actively helped solve the problem and shared great ideas that moved my team forward at every step.	I contributed ideas and helped sometimes but could have done more to support my team consistently.	I struggled to share ideas or help with solving the problem and need to step up my teamwork game.
Communication	I communicated clearly and listened carefully to my team, making sure everyone stayed on the same page.	I communicated okay but sometimes didn't listen or explain my thoughts well enough.	I found it hard to speak up or listen to others during the challenge, which made teamwork difficult.
Problem-Solving Process	I stayed on task and worked with my team through all parts of the challenge, helping us reach a solution.	I helped solve some problems but sometimes lost focus or didn't fully engage with the team.	I was often distracted or didn't take part in solving the problem(s) with my team.
Respect and Support	I respected others' ideas and made my team feel valued and motivated throughout the challenge.	I usually showed respect but didn't always encourage or support my teammates.	I sometimes ignored or dismissed others' ideas and didn't help build a positive team environment.

Speaking and Listening Self-evaluation (Lessons 8 and 18)

Rate your communication skills on a five-star scale. Draw the number of stars you think you earned in each box of the criteria column.

My Name ___			
Criteria	**I Communicated Very Well** *****	**I Communicated Okay** ***	**I Need To Improve My Communication** *
Speaking	I spoke clearly with strong ideas and explanations. I used the right tone and vocabulary for my audience.	I explained my solution but sometimes my ideas were unclear or I didn't use the best words for my audience.	My speaking was unclear/confusing. I struggled to explain my solution well or used the wrong words for my audience.
Listening	I listened carefully to others and used what they said to improve my solution. I showed I understood by asking questions.	I listened to others but sometimes missed important ideas or didn't use their feedback to improve my work.	I didn't listen well to others and/or ignored their ideas when working on my solution.
Nonverbal Communication	I used eye contact, facial expressions, and body language to show I was confident and interested in my topic.	I sometimes used good body language but it wasn't consistent or didn't always match what I was saying.	My body language or facial expressions didn't match my words or made it hard for others to understand my message.
Creativity	I found creative ways to share my solution, making it interesting and easy to follow. I used visuals or examples to help my audience understand.	My presentation had some creative parts, but it could have been more engaging with more examples or visuals.	My presentation was basic and didn't use creative ideas or visuals to help explain my solution.

Creative Thinking Self-evaluation (Lessons 8 and 11)

Draw the emoji face you think you earned in each box of the criteria column.

My Name ______			
Criteria	**3 - Awesome!**	**2 - Getting There**	**1 - Needs Work**
Fluency	I can quickly come up with lots of ideas and keep the activity flowing smoothly.	I come up with a good number of ideas but sometimes get stuck or slow down.	I struggle to think of many ideas and often pause or stop.
Flexibility	I easily switch between different ideas and connect things in new ways.	I can change my thinking sometimes, but it's a bit challenging.	I find it hard to shift ideas or see different connections.
Originality	My ideas are fresh and creative – people might not have thought of them before!	My ideas are somewhat creative but sometimes feel familiar or common.	My ideas are mostly the same as others or not very unique.
Elaboration	I explain my ideas with great detail and examples that make them interesting.	I explain some ideas well, but others need more detail.	My explanations are short or unclear, and I don't give many examples.
Connecting Disparate Objects	I make clever connections between very different things and explain why they fit together or don't belong.	I can connect some different things, but my explanations could be stronger.	I find it hard to connect different objects or explain their relationships.

Questioning Rubric (Lesson 12)

Rate your questioning skills on a five-point scale. Write the number you think you earned in each box of the criteria column.

My Name ______________________________			
Criteria	**3 – I'm an Awesome Detective!**	**2 – I'm On the Case**	**1 – Still a Rookie Sleuth**
Politeness of Questions	I always ask questions politely and respectfully, showing excellent manners that keep the mystery fun and friendly.	I am usually polite with some minor lapses; my questions are generally respectful but could be more courteous.	My questions sometimes sound rude or impatient, which could make the mystery less enjoyable for others.
Use of Deductive Reasoning	I consistently use clues from answers to ask smart, logical next questions that narrow down the mystery person's identity quickly.	I sometimes connect clues and ask logical questions but occasionally miss an opportunity to dig deeper.	I struggle to use clues effectively or ask random questions without a clear logical flow.
Focus on Accomplishments	My questions clearly focus on uncovering the mystery person's accomplishments.	My questions somewhat focus on accomplishments but sometimes get off-topic or vague.	My questions rarely focus on accomplishments and often stray from the assignment's goal.

Teacher Evaluation of Critical Thinking Skills (Lessons 2 and 16)

My Name ________________________________Total Score __________/15

Criteria	3 – Exemplary	2 – Proficient	1 – Developing
Problem Analysis	Thoroughly analyzes the problem, identifying all key aspects and underlying issues with insight and depth.	Analyzes the problem clearly, identifying most key aspects and some underlying issues.	Provides a basic analysis of the problem, missing some important aspects or underlying issues.
Evaluation of Solutions	Evaluates multiple solutions critically, weighing pros and cons effectively and considering long-term impacts.	Evaluates a few solutions with some consideration of pros and cons and short-term impacts.	Evaluates solutions superficially with limited consideration of pros, cons, or impacts.
Selection of Best Solution	Selects the best solution with strong justification supported by logical reasoning and evidence.	Selects a good solution with some justification based on reasoning and evidence.	Selects a solution with minimal justification or reasoning.
Creativity and Innovation	Demonstrates original thinking and creativity in proposing unique or innovative solutions.	Shows some creativity or originality in proposing solutions.	Relies on conventional or obvious solutions with little creativity.
Reflection and Revision	Reflects critically on the chosen solution and suggests thoughtful revisions or improvements.	Reflects on the solution and suggests some revisions or improvements.	Shows limited reflection or does not suggest meaningful revisions.

References

Bennett, A. K. (2012). *Losing grip*. Tate.

Brod, G. (2021). Predicting as a learning strategy. *Psychonomic Bulletin & Review*, *28*(6), 1839–1847.

Callahan, C. M. (2021). Making the grade or achieving the goal?: Evaluating learner and program outcomes in gifted education. In F. A. Karnes & S. M. Bean (Eds.), *Methods and materials for teaching the gifted* (pp. 257–304). Routledge.

Cao, T. H., Jung, J. Y., & Lee, J. (2017). Assessment in gifted education: A review of the literature from 2005 to 2016. *Journal of Advanced Academics*, *28*(3), 163–203.

Carvalho, P. F., Manke, K. J., & Koedinger, K. R. (2018). Not all active learning is equal: Predicting and explaining improves transfer relative to answering practice questions. *Proceedings of the Annual Meeting of the Cognitive Science Society*, *40*.

Dahl, R. (1991). *The Minpins*. Jonathan Cape.

Danielson, C. (2023). *Which one doesn't belong?: A shapes book*. Routledge.

Davis, R. A. (2005). Music education and cultural identity. *Educational Philosophy and Theory*, *37*(1), 47–63.

Einstein, A. (1935). *The world as I see it*. John Lane the Bodley Head.

Ferreri, L., Mas-Herrero, E., Zatorre, R. J., Ripollés, P., Gomez-Andres, A., Alicart, H., Olive, G., Macro-Pallarés, J., Antonijoan, R. M., Valle, M., Riba, J., & Rodriguez-Fornells, A. (2019). Dopamine modulates the reward experiences elicited by music. *Proceedings of the National Academy of Sciences*, *116*(9), 3793–3798.

Fugate, C. M., Behrens, W. A., Boswell, C., & Davis, J. L. (Eds.). (2021). *Culturally responsive teaching in gifted education: Building cultural competence and serving diverse student populations*. Routledge.

Galbraith, J., & Delisle, J. (2015). *When gifted kids don't have all the answers: How to meet their social and emotional needs*. Free Spirit Publishing.

Gallagher, S. A. (2019). Epistemological differences between gifted and typically developing middle school students. *Journal for the Education of the Gifted*, *42*(2), 164–184.

Hammond, Z. (2014). *Culturally responsive teaching and the brain: Promoting authentic engagement and rigor among culturally and linguistically diverse students*. Corwin Press.

Hattie, J., & Timperley, H. (2007). The power of feedback. *Review of Educational Research*, *77*(1), 81–112.

Hess, K. (2025). *Applying depth of knowledge and cognitive rigor: An educator's guide to supporting deeper learning*. Teachers College Press.
Hinton, S. E. (1967). *The outsiders*. Penguin.
Kjellenberg, K., Ekblom, Ö., Tarassova, O., Fernström, M., Nyberg, G., Ekblom, M. M., Helgadóttir, B., & Heiland, E. G. (2024). Short, frequent physical activity breaks improve working memory while preserving cerebral blood flow in adolescents during prolonged sitting – AbbaH teen, a randomized crossover trial. *BMC Public Health*, *24*(1), 2090. https://doi.org/10.1186/s12889-024-19306-y
Kanter, R. M. (1984). *Change masters*. Simon and schuster.
Kaplan, S. N. (2017). Differentiating with depth and complexity. In *Fundamentals of gifted education* (pp. 270–278). Routledge.
Khan, A., Lee, E. Y., & Horwood, S. (2022). Adolescent screen time: associations with school stress and school satisfaction across 38 countries. *European Journal of Pediatrics*, *181*(6), 2273–2281.
Li, M., Zhao, R., Dang, X., Xu, X., Chen, R., Chen, Y., Zhang, Y., Zhao, Z., & Wu, D. (2024). Causal relationships between screen use, reading, and brain development in early adolescents. *Advanced Science*, *11*(11), 2307540.
McCabe, J. A. (2015). Location, location, location! demonstrating the mnemonic benefit of the method of Loci. *Teaching of Psychology*, *42*(2), 169–173. https://doi.org/10.1177/0098628315573143
Neihart, M. (2021). *The social and emotional development of gifted children: What do we know?* Routledge.
Nicholas, M., Skourdoumbis, A., & Bradbury, O. (2024). Meeting the needs and potentials of highability, high-performing, and gifted students via differentiation. *Gifted Child Quarterly*, *68*(2), 154–172.
Park, A. J., Harris, A. Z., Martyniuk, K. M., Chang, C. Y., Abbas, A. I., Lowes, D. C., Kellendonk, C., Gogos, J. A., & Gordon, J. A. (2021). Reset of hippocampal–prefrontal circuitry facilitates learning. *Nature*, *591*(7851), 615–619.
Phillpotts, E. (1918). *A shadow passes*. C. Palmer & Hayward.
Rakow, S. (2021). *Educating gifted students in middle school: A practical guide*. Routledge.
Rayneri, L. J., Gerber, B. L., & Wiley, L. P. (2006). The relationship between classroom environment and the learning style preferences of gifted middle school students and the impact on levels of performance. *Gifted Child Quarterly*, *50*(2), 104–118.
Roberts, J. L., & Inman, T. F. (2023). *Strategies for differentiating instruction: Best practices for the classroom* (4th ed.). Taylor & Francis.
Sibley, B. A., & Etnier, J. L. (2003). The relationship between physical activity and cognition in children: a meta-analysis. *Pediatric Exercise Science*, *15*(3), 243–256.
Silverman, L. K. (2017). The construct of asynchronous development. In *Charting a new course in gifted education* (pp. 36–58). Routledge.
Soderstrom, N. C., Kerr, T. K., & Bjork, R. A. (2016). The critical importance of retrieval – and spacing – for learning. *Psychological Science*, *27*(2), 223–230.
Stewart, T. L. (2007) *The mysterious benedict society*. Little Brown Books for Young Readers.
Thornhill-Miller, B., Camarda, A., Mercier, M., Burkhardt, J. M., Morisseau, T., Bourgeois-Bougrine, S., Vinchon, F., El Hayek, S., Augereau-Landais, M., Mourey, F., Feybesse, C., Sundquist, D., & Lubart, T. (2023). Creativity, critical thinking, communication, and collaboration: Assessment, certification, and promotion of 21st century skills for the future of work and education. *Journal of Intelligence*, *11*(3), 54. https://doi.org/10.3390/jintelligence11030054
Tomlinson, C. A. (2017). Differentiated instruction. In *Fundamentals of gifted education* (pp. 279–292). Routledge.
VanTassel-Baska, J., Hubbard, G. F., & Robbins, J. I. (2020). Differentiation of instruction for gifted learners: Collated evaluative studies of teacher classroom practices. *Roeper Review*, *42*(3), 153–164.

Weinberger, D. (2011). *Too big to know: Rethinking knowledge now that the facts aren't the facts, experts are everywhere, and the smartest person in the room is the room*. Basic Books.
Willis, J. (2008). *Inspiring middle school minds: Gifted, creative, and challenging*. Great Potential Press, Inc.

Recommended Resources

Byrd, I. & Gemert, L. V. (2019). *Gifted guild's guide to depth and complexity*. Self-published.
Inman, T. F. (2023). *Educating the gifted: Wisdom and insights for inspired teaching*. Routledge.
McNair, A. (2019). *A meaningful mess: A teacher's guide to student-driven classrooms, authentic learning, student empowerment, and keeping it all together without losing your mind*. Routledge.
Rakow, S. (2021). *Educating gifted students in middle school: A practical guide*. Routledge.
Visible thinking routines from harvard university's project zero. https://pz.harvard.edu/thinking-routines
Willis, J. (2009). *Inspiring middle school minds: Gifted, creative, & challenging*. Great Potential Press, Inc.

Acknowledgments

To all the educators who recognize and nurture potential in bright children, your patience and love of learning are contagious and made this book worth writing. I am especially grateful to a few special teachers who helped me believe school could be magical. To Claudia Tevis, my first and favorite gifted teacher, this book would never exist without your model of creative and joyful teaching. You taught me to love logic puzzles, long-term projects, and especially solving hands-on spontaneous problems. I am also grateful to the late Mary Foundopoulos, my fifth-grade teacher who differentiated instruction before it was cool. She taught us foreign languages, trigonometry, and allowed me to turn in all my written assignments in code.

Thank you to Rebecca Collazo, Quinn Cowen, and all the staff at Prufrock Press for imagining the possibilities of this new kind of book specifically for middle school gifted teachers. Your vision and insight have shaped this project from a unique presentation into a powerful resource. To all my friends and colleagues in Piper, especially the marvelous and magical Julie Wheeler, thank you for supporting my innovative ideas and for creating a fantastic place to work as an educator. To Sheri Stewart, Connie Phelps, Lindsay Black, and my entire family of KGTC board members who have cheered me on for over a decade, thank you for your commitment to gifted children in Kansas and to creating exciting professional learning for gifted facilitators. To Brandi Klepper, Kris Wiley, Meredith Wisniewski, Jena Randolph, and all my extended gifted family from Missouri, thank you for the laughter, shared wisdom, and constant encouragement. To Candace

Schlein and Loyce Caruthers at the University of Missouri – Kansas City, thank you for showing me that stories about teachers are powerful and important academic work. To my first writing partner and friend Teresa Reddish, your joy and passion for teaching makes me want to keep learning, writing, and caring about the deeper meaning behind every lesson. Tracy Inman, Kathy Nilles, and Lacy Compton at the National Association for Gifted Children, you have been an incredible source of advice and support as I gained the confidence to share my ideas with a wider audience.

To my brilliant, curious, inspiring, and exhausting gifted students past and present. Thank you for pushing me to make our Unique Studies class a surprising new adventure every year. You have truly made this book both magical and real. It is about you, for you, and I hope reading it will bring you a smile full of happy memories.

I am infinitely grateful to my entire family for their love and support over many years of teaching and the most recent months of working on this project. First to my Mom and Dad, your example taught me to value kindness, playfulness, joy, and a lifetime of learning. I am also indebted to each of my younger siblings who endured endless days of playing school with me and who have become inspiring educators and fascinating humans themselves. To my sweet and encouraging parents-in-law who are now watching the completion of this book from heaven, thank you for always believing I was going to accomplish something amazing. Finally, my heart is overflowing with love and gratitude for my extraordinary husband Brett and each of my brilliant daughters, Lilli, Hope, Juliet, and Amelia. You all have sacrificed so many fun times so I could write and waited patiently during endless meetings and emails. You read and revised drafts with me and helped work out the perfect alliterations, examples, and quotes to make this book fun and special. Most of all, you each have a unique and magical giftedness that inspires me daily to make school a better place for wonderful people like you.

About the Author

Jessica LaFollette teaches gifted students at Piper Middle School in Kansas City and is co-chair of the special education department. Dr. LaFollette is also an adjunct professor at the University of Missouri – Columbia where she instructs graduate courses in gifted education. She earned her bachelor's and master's degrees in education from Emporia State University and her PhD from the University of Missouri – Kansas City. She is co-author of the LEAP Guidebook and Modules for Differentiating Instruction for Gifted and High-Potential Students. Dr. LaFollette is a Past President of the Kansas Association for the Gifted, Talented and Creative and past Chair of the National Association for Gifted Children's Parent, Family and Community Network. When she is not teaching, she enjoys puzzles, books, baking, and traveling with her family.

For Product Safety Concerns and Information please contact our EU
representative GPSR@taylorandfrancis.com
Taylor & Francis Verlag GmbH, Kaufingerstraße 24, 80331 München, Germany

www.ingramcontent.com/pod-product-compliance
Lightning Source LLC
Chambersburg PA
CBHW080738300426
44114CB00019B/2619
9781041108634